ACROSS THE BORDER AND BACK

THE TEXAS EXPERIENCE
Books made possible by
Sarah '84 and Mark '77 Philpy

ACROSS the BORDER and BACK

Music in the Big Bend

Marcia Hatfield Daudistel
Photographs by Bill Wright
Foreword by W. K. Stratton

TEXAS A&M UNIVERSITY PRESS | COLLEGE STATION

This paper meets the requirements of ANSI/NISO Z39.48–1992 (Permanence of Paper).

Binding materials have been chosen for durability.

Manufactured in China through Martin Book Management

LIBRARY OF CONGRESS CATALOGING-IN-PUBLICATION DATA

NAMES: Daudistel, Marcia Hatfield, author. | Wright, Bill, 1933– photographer (expression) |
Stratton, W. K., 1955– writer of foreword.

TITLE: Across the border and back: music in the Big Bend / Marcia Hatfield Daudistel;
photographs by Bill Wright; foreword by W.K. Stratton.

OTHER TITLES: Texas experience (Texas A & M University. Press)

DESCRIPTION: First edition. | College Station: Texas A&M University Press, [2022] |
Series: The Texas experience

IDENTIFIERS: LCCN 2021020082 | ISBN 9781623499440 (cloth) | ISBN 9781623499457 (ebook)

SUBJECTS: LCSH: Popular music—Texas—Big Bend Region—History and criticism. |
Musicians—Texas—Big Bend Region. | Popular music—Mexico—Ojinaga—
History and criticism. | Musicians—Mexico—Ojinaga.

CLASSIFICATION: LCC ML3477.7.T35 D38 2022 | DDC 781.6409764/93—dc23

LC RECORD available at https://lccn.loc.gov/2021020082

It never got too weird for me.

— Artist BOYD ELDER (1944–2018), on touring with the Eagles

CONTENTS

MET LOUIS AND FRANCES COZBY when I was a nit of a newspaper reporter in the short-grass country of the far northeastern corner of Comancheria. The Cozbys were a part of that now vanished breed known as itinerant journalists; they worked their way from one small town paper in the West and Southwest to another, never staying anywhere for long. They stood out in the town where they eventually landed, Guthrie, Oklahoma. They had traveled much of the world as *Stars and Stripes* scribes during World War II. Their politics were socialist; they were just shy of being fellow travelers. I always thought of them as characters who'd escaped from a John Steinbeck novel. They were a childless couple by choice, and they sort of halfway adopted me when I was a kid trying to learn the newspaper business. I have many fond memories of dinners at their book-filled cabin tucked into a stretch of woods along the Cimarron River.

Both Louis and Frances had graduated from J-school at the University of Oklahoma. One of their classmates had gone on to become the managing editor of the *Kansas City Star* back when it was one of America's great newspapers. When he retired, he escaped to Alpine, Texas, and moved into a primitive adobe dwelling, which was just about as far removed from a metropolitan city room as he could get. Each November, the Cozbys loaded up Louis's battered pickup and made the long voyage south and west to celebrate Thanksgiving with their friend. They returned loaded down with stories and photos of a land of mountains, desert, and highly individualistic people. Those stories became my introduction to the Big Bend country.

It took years before I was able to visit the place myself. In the meantime, as I heard and read more about it, the whole of Far West Texas became a kind of mythic locale for me. When I did begin making journeys to the part of Texas that is "west of West Texas" twenty years or so ago, I found it more intriguing than I ever imagined it could be. Several authors have given me insight I otherwise wouldn't have. Among them are my friend Marcia Hatfield Daudistel and her frequent collaborator Bill Wright.

Marcia grew up in Louisiana amid swamps and bayous, likely never dreaming she would find herself a publisher, editor, and writer in the Trans-Pecos region of Texas. In addition to her own work at Texas Western Press, her husband, Howard Daudistel, was a dean, senior executive vice president, and provost at the University of Texas at El Paso, so El Paso and Far West Texas, including the Big Bend country, became her home turf. While she saw more than seventy books into print during her time at Texas Western, Marcia is relatively new to the business of being an author herself. Over a recent breakfast in Albuquerque, she told me that she credits Wright as one of the people who encouraged her (goaded her?) into taking pen in hand herself. She "got" the cultural nuances of her adopted homeland. She put that understanding to use when books under her name began to be published.

She received well-deserved kudos when she edited *Literary El Paso*, which, for my money, is the best entry in Texas Christian University Press's literary cities series. She gathered outstanding writing, both historical and contemporary, to forge this compelling written portrait of El Paso. The book is bilingual and features pieces written by people from all parts of the city's cultural spectrum. She also edited *Grace & Gumption*, a book about El Paso women, as well as cowrote *The Women of Smeltertown*, concerning women who lived and raised families at the city's notorious smelter owned by the American Smelting and Refining Company.

Wright is from West Texas (Abilene). For years after graduating from the University of Texas at Austin, he was a businessman. Then, in 1989, he sold the company he had cofounded, Western Marketing, and was able to free himself from the nine-to-five world and focus his talents on photography, research, and writing. He took deep dives into his subject matter. For his book *The Tiguas: Pueblo Indians of Texas*, he devoted six years to research, shooting photographs, collecting other images from tribal members, and creating an extensive bibliography. Texas Western Press at the University of Texas at El Paso published his book. Marcia was the associate director at Texas Western, and as his publisher, she developed a professional relationship with Wright that has continued with the publication of the book you now have in hand.

Wright, too, kept busy as a chronicler of life and history on the border and elsewhere in Texas. *Portraits from the Desert: Bill Wright's Big Bend* is a collection of his photographs and writings about the Big Bend country spanning some fifty years; he made his first visit there in 1950. He also authored or collaborated on books dealing with the Kickapoos in Texas, ranching in the Big Bend, and a biography of Maggie Smith, a border legend who was a doctor, lawyer, banker, self-appointed justice of the peace, herbalist, coroner, and all-around character who worked on both sides of the Rio Grande in the 1940s and 1950s.

One day Marcia was driving east from El Paso toward the Big Bend country. She passed through Valentine and was astonished by what she didn't see: any human beings, absolutely none. Valentine is the only incorporated municipality in the whole of Jeff Davis County (the county seat, Fort Davis, is unincorporated), yet it seemed to have no people, at least at that given moment. Still, she knew people lived in Valentine as well as in the rest of the Big Bend country. What kind of people would call this place home? Thus germinated the book she coauthored with Wright, *Authentic Texas: People of the Big Bend*, which was published in 2013. Illustrated with Wright's superb photographs, the written profiles by Marcia and Wright of a wide range of Far West Texas inhabitants became a favorite of mine. Six years later, I find myself frequently pulling it down from the shelf to thumb through it.

Now the Daudistel-Wright collaboration, with Marcia's text and Bill's photographs, has produced this book, *Across the Border and Back*. It's an ideal complement to *Authentic Texas: People of the Big Bend*. If the earlier book creates a kind of tapestry of people of different ages, experiences, and ethnicities, this one brings together a number of different musical genres into a kind of suite. The sounds are diverse yet singular. Musicians in the Big Bend have to be competent in a number of musical styles if they want to find work. "In the Big Bend," Marcia writes, "the musicians ask the question when being hired: 'What kind of music do you want?'" It could be conjunto one night, country-western the next, and rock and roll on the weekend. Whatever the form, there does seem to be a consistent sort of soulful feel to Big Bend sounds reflective of the territory the musicians call home.

At some point early on, Marcia and Bill determined that they wouldn't limit themselves to interviews and photographs from the American side of the Rio Grande. They spent time in the area known as La Junta de los Ríos, sometimes referred to as "the Devil's Swing." It is the region in Mexico where the two primary rivers of the Chihuahuan Desert, the Rio Conchos and the Rio Grande, merge just upstream from the cities of Ojinaga, Chihuahua, and Presidio, Texas. It is a fertile area, as desert country goes. Human beings have continuously occupied it for some eight thousand years. Some of the most compelling interviews and photographs come from Marcia's and Wright's excursions into that ancient place.

I like song lyrics included here that have come from the Big Bend country, in particular Sunny Ozuna's "Reina de Mi Amor" (Queen of My Love). "Sin ti, yo no puedo vivir / Yo no puedo existir / Por lo tanto que te quiero . . ." These words carry an impact in Spanish that's lost when translated into English. Ozuna, credited as being the father of música tejana,

has been in my pantheon of Texas music heroes for quite some time. I associate him with San Antonio, where he was born and still resides. But as you will learn from *Across the Border and Back*, he and his bands have played regularly in the Trans-Pecos for three generations now. The Big Bend country is far removed from San Antonio's urban West Side, but Ozuna's sound is very much part of the soundtrack of that vast landscape.

You never know who you might turn up in Big Bend country. Flatlander and photographer Butch Hancock, who wrote "Boxcars"—sometimes I think it's my all-time favorite song—and many other great tunes, led raft tours on the Rio Grande. Drummer and songwriter Doyle Bramhall lived out his final days in Alpine. He was arguably best known for his collaborations with Stevie Ray Vaughan. And in a six-degrees-of-separation kind of thing, you will learn from this book that Michael Stevens, who built guitars for Vaughan, Eric Clapton, and others, lives and works outside Alpine to this day.

Across the Border and Back takes the reader on an insightful journey to a place whose sonic wonders rival the visual. We're lucky we have Marcia Hatfield Daudistel and Bill Wright doing the work they do. Their new book is one I know my old friends Louis and Frances Cozby would have loved.

—W. K. Stratton

ACROSS THE BORDER AND BACK

Craig Carter.

Introduction

THERE IS A VAST, remote, sparsely populated area of breathtaking beauty in far southwest Texas along the US-Mexico border known as the Big Bend. This region and farther west to El Paso is where Texas keeps its mountains. It can be startling to come from the plains of the Panhandle or the rolling hills of Austin and the Hill Country and be suddenly surrounded by majestic mountains.

The people who live in the towns of the Texas Big Bend—Terlingua, Fort Davis, Marfa, Alpine, Marathon, Balmorhea, and Presidio—are passionate about this place they chose to make their home. Some who were raised in the area never left. Some tried to leave but returned. Many new residents have come here. All, both long-timers and newcomers, have been seduced by the peace, quiet, and small-town atmosphere in the Big Bend. It's an entirely different way of life. In fact, most of those who left and stayed gone decided that the very things that drew them there were just too inconvenient.

The positive side is there is no urban sprawl or big-box stores. There are no traffic jams unless you have to wait for javelina or deer to cross the road. You can make a U-turn in the middle of the street without a problem. However, there are also no malls, Starbucks, or fast-food restaurants, except for the lone McDonald's in Alpine, the home of Sul Ross State University. Retirees soon find that if they need specialized medical help, there is only limited medical and dental care. Real estate prices are high, though not in comparison to Dallas, Houston, or Austin.

The Big Bend music scene is well known. Terlingua, in particular, attracts musicians from all over the state. Alpine is a convenient stopover for touring musicians on national tours, and local bands and performers frequently draw large crowds. Musicians who come to live in the Big Bend are passionate about living here. Although there may be more opportunity for gigs in larger cities, they stay here, working other jobs to support themselves and their families while performing when they can, sometimes just for gas money. The norteño and conjunto music of Mexico have infused much of the music that is performed here.

This makes sense, because along the Texas-Mexico border, crossing over into either country was once an everyday occurrence for many people. The nightlife of Ciudad Juárez, Mexico, the largest city on the

US-Mexico border, regularly drew the residents of El Paso and tourists alike across the international bridge. The people of both cities shopped, worked, and visited physicians, dentists, and family members in both countries. This was also true of the Big Bend, but the border there was not fenced or clearly marked in some places. That has changed since 9/11, and the heightened security has made informal crossing impossible. Previously the people of Presidio, Redford, Terlingua, and Lajitas were able to simply wade across the Rio Grande when the water level was low or cross by rowboat to work, shop, visit family, or hear musicians from both sides. Those days are over, but the cultural influences from both sides of the border are embedded in the region.

In Texas, regional music typically blends the music brought into an area by settlers, soldiers, cowboys, and early European immigrants, all influencing the music of a particular region. Instruments that were unfamiliar at first are incorporated into the music. For example, the accordion, originally brought to south-central Texas by German immigrants, became a key instrument in norteño music.

The music of the Texas-Mexico border includes the music of the Rio Grande Valley, El Paso, and the Big Bend and is often referred to as borderlands music. Musicians on the US side of the border learned and played the music of Mexico, while musicians from Mexico learned to play the music from the US side of the border. Such binationality makes borderlands music unique. In the Big Bend, the characteristics of this regional, binational music are defined by the musicians themselves. In their interviews, they share their background stories and the variations they bring to the music they perform. The songwriters frequently compose in both Spanish and English—just one more element that helps define borderlands music.

Radios, record players, and jukeboxes brought the music of the nation to this remote area. Eduardo Alvarez remembers Mexican musicians playing on the Marfa Air Field Base when he was a teenager during World War II and playing in various pickup bands. The Mexican American musicians on the Texas side and the musicians in Mexico learned the popular music played on the US side of the border. So, in addition to the music of Mexico he performed for events such as weddings, quinceañeras, and parties in the Big Bend, Eduardo also learned to play the big band music of that era.

Country-western is also a major genre in the Big Bend and was the only music played on the radio station in Alpine until the late 1960s: the classic country music of Patsy Cline, Porter Wagoner, Conway Twitty, and others well known from the Grand Ole Opry. This music is still played on both sides of the border, along with contemporary country music. With the emergence of rock and roll, the teenagers of the area welcomed the limited play time allowed for their music on the local radio station. Young musicians began playing the music they would hear on their transistor radios from stations as far away as Oklahoma City and as near as the radio station in Ojinaga, Mexico, and from Wolfman Jack, broadcasting from XERF-AM in Acuña, Mexico. Rock and roll bands performed at high school events and at events attracting students from Sul Ross State University, earning them a local following among the teenagers of the Big Bend. Top 40 hits did not homogenize the music of the region but rather added a new dimension by introducing new instruments to the traditional music of the border.

The music of Mexico has many classifications, but conjunto, norteño, Tejano, and the Ojinaga Sound are the main genres heard in the Big Bend. The instruments help define the genres, and the types of songs vary from polka derivatives to corridos. This music, popular in Mexico, became popular across the border as well. For the families who were originally citizens of Mexico generations ago, it was the nostalgic sound heard in the homes of grandparents and parents and at celebrations.

Responding to the demand for norteño, conjunto, and Tejano music, the rock and roll and

Matt Skinner and Jim Wilson.

country-western bands also played *cumbias* and performed songs from Mexico. The Mexican musicians responded to the demand for country-western music by playing Bob Wills and his Texas swing, Hank Williams, Willie Nelson, and current country hits.

The musicians interviewed in this book live or have lived in the Big Bend communities of Alpine, Marfa, Fort Davis, Presidio, Marathon, and Terlingua as well as in Ojinaga, Mexico. In fact, for the musicians in Ojinaga who play the Ojinaga Sound, an iconic innovation of the music of Mexico, our interviews were their first opportunity to speak to a larger audience about their music. They were grateful to be asked to tell their stories, and it was a privilege for us to hear them.

Though he does not live in the Big Bend, Sunny Ozuna, of Sunny and the Sunliners, has a place here with others such as Little Joe y la Familia and Ruben Ramos and the Mexican Revolution who have toured this region for decades. His 1963 hit "Talk to Me" went to number 11 on the national Billboard charts, making an important bridge between Tejano and pop music and drawing Big Bend audiences of Mexican Americans, Mexicans, and Anglos that included teenagers, grandparents, and parents. He brought a nationally known Tejano-English music blend to an area where norteño was the most popular music from Mexico.

All the musicians interviewed perform throughout the Big Bend and are not tied to a particular community except by residence. Once the initial interviews were scheduled, word of mouth spread about the book, and the musicians suggested others for us to contact.

Some of the musicians can make their living by music alone; others work at other jobs: blacksmiths, ranchers, teachers, river raft guides, and hatmakers. The musicians of the Big Bend also tour in Texas and sometimes nationally. They tell stories of how they developed a passion for music at an early age and made a lifelong commitment to performing, writing, and playing. They also share their passion for the Big Bend and why they chose to live in an area lacking the amenities that even most small cities have. We also interviewed the owners of clubs and other venues in the Big Bend that feature musical acts, both local and national. We talked to radio show hosts, an iconic guitar maker, and cowboy poets. The book also contains a section of original songs written by the musicians in both Spanish and English and a discography of the CDs produced by bands on both sides of the border.

Choosing to live in the Big Bend to pursue a life in music can be difficult, although local music is very popular here. The musicians have come to the Big Bend from all over the United States to make their homes and follow their dreams. These are their stories.

—Marcia Hatfield Daudistel

The Music of Mexico on the Border

SEVERAL TYPES OF MUSIC originated in Mexico that, over time, blended with the music of Texas while retaining their roots in Mexico. The instruments played define each of these types of music. The music of Mexico most commonly played in the Big Bend can be divided into the main genres of conjunto, Tejano, and norteño music.

Conjunto

The word *conjunto* means "small group." This music, originally a blend of Mexican music with the polka music and waltzes from the German and Czech immigrants in Central Texas, began in the late 1800s in South and Central Texas and San Antonio. The instruments played in conjunto are the accordion and the twelve-string bass, the *bajo sexto*. Conjunto soon added the electric bass and drum. This was the music of working-class Tejanos, played in agricultural camps, remote ranches, and small communities in southeast and southwest Texas for dances, parties, and celebrations. Conjunto is frequently compared to "hillbilly," the music of working-class Anglos in the South, or folk music in the United States.

When diatonic or German-style accordions with one row of ten buttons became readily available, they were ideal for musicians at the time. They produce great sound, are lightweight, and are low in cost. In the 1890s, conjunto musicians began adding a small drum called a tambora to the accordion and bajo sexto.

Narciso Martinez is considered to be the father of modern conjunto and is also called "El Huracán del Valle" (The Hurricane of the Valley). Santiago Jiménez Sr., another conjunto pioneer, was a songwriter and the maestro of the two-row button accordion, which became popular in the 1930s, a time of innovation in conjunto. Jiménez also added a *toloche*, a contrabass that became popular until the 1950s, when the electric bass replaced it. His sons Santiago Jiménez Jr. and Flaco Jiménez carry on his conjunto tradition.

When Valerio Longoria, another pioneer in conjunto, added vocals to the accordion, interest in singing accompanied by the accordion increased. Female vocalists such as Lydia Mendoza became popular in the 1930s, and female duets became popular in the 1950s. In 2013, the first all-female band, Grupo Imagen from Corpus Christi, joined other Tejanas to perform at the Tejano Conjunto Festival in 2015.

Tony de la Rosa was heavily influenced by country music and western swing. He introduced the amplified bajo sexto and bass, also changing the polka tempo by slowing it down from traditional polkas. He added horns in the 1960s and was the first to use a drum set. He played a three-row, three-key accordion.

Gilberto Perez has performed for forty years and has an unmistakable style of combining his alto vocals in a duet with a second voice. He is a staunch advocate for conjunto music and its preservation. Over time, he has incorporated other instruments into his music but has never wavered from classic conjunto: accordion, drums, bajo sexto, and electric bass. Ruben Vela, Perez, and Tony de la Rosa toured during agricultural seasons, following the migrant families from South Texas west to California and other states to perform the music the workers loved.

Contemporary conjunto bands include the Hometown Boys, Esteban "Steve" Jordan, and Jaime y los Chamacos. Conjunto Primavera from Ojinaga, Chihuahua, Mexico, are pioneers in developing the distinctive "Ojinaga Sound."

Conjunto is waning in popularity, and some fear it will fade away, giving way to norteño-style music. There are conjunto fans who are purists, and equally impassioned followers who are contemporary conjunto fans. It is not as popular in the Big Bend as norteño music. Other types of music influenced by conjunto are mariachi, banda, and techno-banda.

Norteño

The differences between conjunto and norteño can be confusing. The defining difference is that conjunto is uniquely Mexican American and norteño is Mexican. Both types of music are from northern Mexico, but conjunto blends a German influence into the music. Both use the same four instruments, the accordion and bajo sexto with the addition of drums and electric bass. Both came to being in the Rio Grande borderlands in the late 1800s and are identified as the original binational sound of the border. The German polkas and waltzes in conjunto and the Mexican ranchera music and corridos sung in Spanish in norteño are the defining characteristics of each genre. New listeners may find them identical.

According to the article "Get Your Norteño out of My Conjunto" by Saul Elbein in the *Texas Observer* on May 20, 2011, "norteño is faster, with a more insistent beat; conjunto is slower, more like a polka. Norteño, by contrast, tends to be built around the *corrido*. *Corridos* are an ancient form of ballad, going back to Spain, which tell the story of some person, place or event."

There are historical corridos in conjunto, as well as in norteño. A new type of corrido, the *narcocorrido* or *traficante corrido*, tells stories of drug trafficking along the border. Cartel bosses have sometimes hired songwriters to compose corridos about them. This music most closely resembles hip-hop and rap. Attempts to ban these songs from radio play have been largely unsuccessful. Since these songs tell the story of how poor, even destitute people are driven to drug trafficking, a few of them have become theme songs of this music. They are also popular with people who have no connection with any of the cartels or gangs, in the same way that not everyone who listens to so-called gangsta rap is actually a member of a street gang.

Prominent norteño musicians and groups come from California as well as Texas and other states in Mexico. Ramón Ayala, called the "Accordion King," teamed with Cornelio Reyna and began Relámpagos del Norte. When Reyna passed away, the band became known as Los Bravos del Norte, billed as Ramón Ayala y Sus Bravos del Norte. He continues an active touring and recording schedule.

Los Tigres del Norte, from San Diego, are Grammy Award winners and were number 1 on the Billboard Latin Chart in 1964. Other well-known norteño musicians are Los Huracanes del Norte; Los Rieleros del Norte, founded in Pecos, Texas; and Intocable from Zapata, Texas.

Mexican Americans make a clear distinction between themselves and the people of Mexico who come to the United States. Norteño music is more popular with the people of Mexico, while Mexican Americans want conjunto and Tejano music, which is slowly disappearing from radio play. Conjunto and Tejano are uniquely Texan, and there is concern they will fade away.

Tejano

Tejano music began in Texas and was first known as Tex-Mex. When conjunto and folk music began to gather inspiration from the fusion of rock and roll, R&B, and doo-wop in the 1950s and 1960s, this new genre was born. Tejano occasionally incorporates the accordion but typically uses drums, electric guitar, and a brass section and emphasizes synthesizers.

Sunny Ozuna of Sunny and the Sunliners is a pioneer of Tejano music. Influenced by the popular music of the 1950s and 1960s, his group added Spanish lyrics to those songs. They also added synthesizers to their music.

Little Joe and the Latinairs, now La Familia, introduced an orchestral sound. In the 1970s and 1980s, Rudy Valdez and Espejismo from McAllen and Grupo Mazz from Brownsville added a keyboard during the era of disco music.

The orchestral type of Tejano music adds brass, a dominant feature, and the occasional use of the accordion. Some examples of orchestral bands are the Liberty Band, Latin Breed, and Ruben Ramos and the Texas Revolution.

Other types within this category include urban Tejano, pop, and progressive. The modern bands include La Mafia, Los Palominos, Grupo Limite, and La Sombra.

It would be impossible to have a rational discussion of Tejano music without talking about Selena Quintanilla, the "Queen of Tejano Music." Born in Lake Jackson, Texas, in 1971, she still exerts a strong

Musicians of Ojinaga, Chihuahua, Mexico.

Bill Wright; Mike Davidson; Abraham Baeza, Cultural Affairs, City of Ojinaga, Chihuahua, Mexico; Marcia Hatfield Daudistel; John Ferguson, mayor of Presidio, Texas.

influence even after her death in 1995. She began performing with her group Selena y los Dinos, which included her older brother AB and her sister Suzette. At that time, Tejano music was male-dominated, but that barrier was overcome when her hit album *Entre a Mi Mundo* was number 1 on the Regional Mexican Albums Billboard chart. A single from that album, "Como la Flor," became her signature song. As a breakthrough female Tejano artist, she made fashion choices that led to her being called the Tejano Madonna. Her birthday is now Selena Day in Texas, ordered by then governor George W. Bush. Selena sold over sixty-five million albums, making her the best-selling Latin music female artist in history.

Flaco Jiménez, Doug Sahm, and Augie Meyers of the Tex-Mex Revue, now known as the Texas Tornados, combine the elements of conjunto with country, rock and roll, and R&B. Jiménez also plays the conjunto accordion. Sahm and Meyers, working with collaborators Freddy Fender and Jiménez, released hit albums, and all went on to great success. Jiménez has played with Dwight Yoakam and the Rolling Stones, among others. Meyers has played with Bob Dylan and the Allman Brothers. Freddy Fender rose to fame with his songs "Wasted Days and Wasted Nights" and "Before the Next Teardrop Falls."

Sahm and Meyers were also in the popular 1960s group the Sir Douglas Quintet. Meyers on the Vox organ provided a feature sound of that band.

Intocable from Zapata, Texas, offer a unique fusion of Tejano and norteño music with a pop influence from new contemporary artists. They remain one of most well-known groups nationally and in Texas.

The Texas Tornados, along with other prominent contemporary Tejano artists, brought the Tejano sound to national attention, and Tejano music remains popular, particularly in Central and South Texas, although norteño music is more popular along the border in El Paso and the Big Bend because more people from northern Mexico are now living in the United States.

2

The Ojinaga Sound

A PARTICULAR TYPE OF MUSIC found on the border in the Big Bend is called the Ojinaga Sound, a well-known variation of norteño music that began in Ojinaga, Mexico, and is closely identified with the city of Ojinaga and the state of Chihuahua. This original sound is distinctive because of the addition of the saxophone to norteño music and because of its improvisational style. The musicians of Ojinaga are justifiably proud to perform this music, the sound of their home.

We made three trips to Ojinaga, which flows nearly seamlessly into Presidio, Texas, in Presidio County. According to 2017 census figures, Presidio has a population of 4,099 and Ojinaga has a population of 28,040. It is immediately apparent that Ojinaga is the much larger city, with its increased traffic and greater number of shops and restaurants. It is a colorful place with brightly painted buildings, and restaurants that feature strolling musicians. Before the days of heightened security at the border checkpoint, the citizens of both cities crossed the border on nearly a daily basis. They function as sister cities, with the Presidio Fire Department assisting with fires in Ojinaga, and the Ojinaga Fire Department coming to fight fires in Presidio and the surrounding small towns. There is

more medical care and shopping for the people and tourists of Presidio available in Ojinaga.

Presidio mayor John Ferguson, an accomplished musician, along with his assistant at City Hall and our translator, Stephanie Lares, who lives in Ojinaga and works in Presidio, and musician Mike Davidson of Los Pinche Gringos accompanied us to Ojinaga. Abraham Baeza Tarango, assistant to the mayor of Ojinaga and a sort of cultural liaison who is now the director of Parque de Aventura Barrancas del Cobre, met us at Ojinaga City Hall. Announcements had gone out on the local radio station for musicians in Ojinaga to come to City Hall to be interviewed for this book. Ojinaga is a "music town," and bronze stars that look like the ones on the Hollywood Walk of Fame in Los Angeles are set into the walkways and lobby of the municipal building, honoring musicians and bands from Ojinaga. We learned that there is a small monument in town to Conjunto Primavera, one of the pioneer groups of the Ojinaga Sound.

We were told again and again that no one had ever asked the musicians for their stories, although this style of music is well known in Mexico and the state of Chihuahua. All the musicians, whether older, middle

Julio Ramirez plays and sings in Ojinaga City Hall.

aged, or young, are committed to preserving their unique style of music.

We made two more trips to Ojinaga, one to conduct more interviews and one to photograph the groups and individuals. We received CDs that they had recorded, publicity stills, and website addresses for the groups. The musicians themselves explained the Ojinaga Sound, the soundtrack of their lives.

Abraham welcomed us into a large conference room with portraits of former mayors lining the walls. There was a table with various flavors of agua fresca, pan dulce and other pastries, coffee, and water for us all. Soon, nearly twenty local musicians filed

into the room. There were solo acts as well as bands. The atmosphere became lively when we began interviewing Julio Ramirez, one of the oldest musicians at seventy-three. He proudly brought his accordion, an instrument that was obviously well used and well loved. We asked whether he would consider playing something for everyone. Without hesitation, he stood to play and sing a norteño ballad in a beautiful full voice. Office workers were lured to the conference room to listen; the group came to their feet cheering.

After Julio Ramirez played, he sat down to be interviewed. He was born in Durango, Mexico, and was part of the group Guerrilleros de Chihuahua for forty-two years, known in the United States as the Guerrilleros. The group members were originally from Durango, where they were based, and then they were in Chihuahua for eleven years until 1973, when they came to Ojinaga. They toured the United States with stops in Kansas, Phoenix, San Antonio, and other locations. The five members of the group played accordion, bajo sexto, bass, saxophone, and the drums: classic norteño music, with the addition of the saxophone.

"We came in 1973, so we were the first norteño music[ians] living here in Ojinaga. We decided to bring this to Ojinaga because there were no other bands doing that. There was no norteño music here. There was only *orquestra* and mariachi music," Julio said. Los Rebeldes and Conjunto Primavera were among the earliest groups to develop the Ojinaga Sound. Julio's group added the saxophone, inspired by its sound. Julio remembers that this new sound was popular right away. The group recorded twelve LPs. Julio has played the accordion for so many years, he doesn't remember when he began playing.

Julio retired from the group when he was ready to stop performing after decades on the road. Observing increased drug use, promiscuity, and alcohol abuse, he felt that life on the road was in direct conflict with his religious beliefs and family values. "I saw very bad things being involved in music like drugs, women, and alcohol," he said. Now he plays his accordion in church with a chorale on Sundays. "I saw so many things being a musician, I think God has prepared something else for music, what I am doing now. I feel more comfortable now at the church than what I was doing before," he said.

David Tavarez, seventy-seven, has retired from music. His major instrument was the slide trombone. When he was in elementary school in the 1950s he began a musical group in Ojinaga. He did not grow up in a musical family; he was the only one to play instruments. David retired from working for Mexican Customs after thirty-one years.

"I was not influenced by an artist because I think that before, it was just instrumental. The other groups from the area influenced me. There was no singing, just instrumental." He recalls playing Glenn Miller, which is still heard in Ojinaga because it is dance music that is familiar to the older people. "We did not have a lot of norteño going before the sixties. The only music that they would hear more were boleros, or waltzes," he said.

David was there when the Ojinaga Sound was taking root and being defined as unique from other norteño, Tejano, and conjunto music. "It started bit by bit. It spread until everybody started liking and dancing norteño," he said. He played with the pioneer groups of the Ojinaga Sound and the Chente Orchestra and was a member of the orchestra Shume Guevara, also playing with Beto Franco.

José Martin Herrera Olivas, also known as Martin Herrera, began playing the guitar at the age of nine. "The guitar is what made me feel the music. That is the main instrument to start playing," he said. Martin now plays the saxophone, accordion, and bajo sexto. He was with Grupo Amanecer, which was started in 1984, for twenty-one years. He is now with the group Dominantes de Ojinaga.

He started his own recording studio in La Mula on the way to Chihuahua, only forty minutes from Ojinaga. "I'm recording other bands from Chihuahua and from here in Ojinaga. I make their CDs," Martin said.

His favorite song to perform is "El Moño Negro" (The Black Ribbon). "That's the best song that I feel comfortable playing because the group has a lot of fun pleasing the people," he said. "They recognize that we're from Ojinaga."

The music he grew up listening to with his parents and grandparents was that of Marco Antonio Solís, who began performing at the age of six and went on to win Grammys and a star on the Hollywood Walk of Fame. Martin will sing these songs, performing them in norteño style. He is now in production with Dominantes de Ojinaga on a new CD.

David Tavarez (*left*) and Samuel Aguillera of Maximo Norte (*right*).

Another member of Dominantes de Ojinaga, Victor Muruato, plays the bass. He began playing the guitar at the age of fourteen, influenced by his mother. "My mom used to play the accordion, the guitar, and the toloche. It's like a big, big guitar, it stands on the floor, it looks like a violin," Victor said. He was raised with all types of music, including the Beatles, but decided to concentrate on the Ojinaga Sound because he was born and raised in Ojinaga. He is another musician who makes his living through his music.

José Torres, one of the five members of the Bandoleros group, began playing his guitar in church, inspired by the musicians who played on Sunday. "I saw the guys playing the instruments at church, so that's where I started. My grandpa played the *guitarra quinta*," he said. It is a small Mexican guitar

played in trios, so José grew up hearing the norteño style. He further defined the distinctive Ojinaga Sound. "It's the bajo sexto, which is a twelve-string guitar, but it can be used almost to accompany itself. We have the bajo sexto, the accordion, the alto sax, electric bass, drum set, and the singer, of course," he explained. José believes there is a major difference in the singing style, featuring mostly high notes.

Mike Davidson added his definition: "Well, it's just the sax, and the accordion does fills. The accordion takes the basic tone, the saxophone takes the alto part, one step above, and they just follow the same melody and do these really quick, intricate duets, it's really infectious," he said. "Like a sixteenth-note run, and they're always a third or a sixth apart," added John Ferguson.

José started a rock band in Ojinaga but found that the locals did not like it and he had difficulty finding musicians to play. He is more attracted to norteño. "Rock is slower, I'm more norteño, rock is done," he said. John Ferguson added, "Speaking from experience because we see each other, there are people in Ojinaga who like to play rock, but it's going to be for a very limited audience. If you're playing rock to make money, forget it."

When he began playing norteño, Torres began playing the bajo sexto. "It's different because to play the bajo sexto, I have to have a lot of emotion, to feel it. I am trying to get used to it, but I'm not there yet, not where I want to be," he said.

The song they perform to get everyone out on the dance floor is "Se Va Muriendo Mi Alma," made famous by Marco Antonio Solís and also recorded by Ramiro Valenzuela. His favorite song to play is "Fuerte No Soy" by Intocable, the famous Tejano/norteño band from Zapata, Texas. "We're not one hundred percent norteño," José said. "We're implementing banda, the orchestra, to the norteño, because that is what is popular for the young audience right now." John added, "In place of the electric bass they have a tuba, that's like with the banda. So it is norteño banda."

Banda is over one hundred years old and is reminiscent of the German brass bands also called bandas. "I've got a recording with a group from LA called Banda de Los Muertos and they play a bunch of traditional songs but it's got the finest brass parts. I'm kind of taken aback by the modern banda because those guys are dressed in red leather chaps," said Mike.

José proudly showed us a video on his phone of one of their performances to standing, cheering crowds. The Bandoleros prove that the genres of border music continue to evolve and change and their innovation to the Ojinaga Sound is a success.

Grupo Veneno de Ojinaga is a group consisting of five members of the Chavez family. Mario Chavez plays the electric bass guitar and is first voice, Brandon Chavez is on drums, Bernardo Chavez plays the bajo sexto, Luis Mario Chavez plays accordion and is second voice, and Marco Chavez plays the saxophone.

Based in Ojinaga, they play in small towns in Chihuahua and other states in Mexico. Their favorite song to play is "Disculpe Usted," and the cumbia they play to get everyone on the dance floor is one written by Mario and his wife, "Los Dichos de Don Pepe."

Mario knows the Ojinaga Sound is recognizable: "Yes, when we are playing in other states for example, people will say, 'Oh, they're from Ojinaga,' when they start listening, because of the music we play. They will know," he said. Mario was born in Parras but came to Ojinaga at the age of two and was influenced by the most famous band in the history of the Ojinaga Sound, Conjunto Primavera. "It was local music that I used to hear when I was young because my grandfather liked that type of music. We are surrounded by that," he said. The group plays at events such as weddings and quinceañeras as well as performance venues.

Bernardo Chavez began playing with the group at the age of seven. He is now thirteen. Brandon Chavez also began playing with the group at a young age. Music is a well-established family tradition.

True to the Ojinaga Sound, they also update their music to reflect a younger, more popular taste while staying true to their sound. For their older fans, they play music from the Mexican artist Emmanuel, popular in the 1970s and 1980s.

Raymundo Sanchez, Ricardo Lozano, Juan Dominguez, Everardo Velazquez, and Lino Soto of the band Declaración Norteña de Ojinaga also came to be interviewed. The band members live in Ojinaga, raising families in their hometown.

Raymundo was born in Delicias, Chihuahua, but began playing in Denton, Texas. He returned to Ojinaga, where he was raised, because his entire family lives there.

Raymundo also works in construction in the area when he is not touring. "I was with another group but was invited to be part of this band, so we made a new group," Raymundo said. Declaracíon Norteña is now

@GVenenoojinaga   Grupo Veneno de Ojinaga   626-499-7427   grupovenenodeojinaga

Publicity flier for Grupo Veneno. *Left to right*: Marco Chavez, Luis Mario Chavez, Brandon Chavez, Mario Chavez, and Bernardo Chavez.

limited to performing in Mexico because they lack the visas to perform in the United States, even in adjacent Presidio, Texas. They stay busy performing in Durango and in most states in Mexico.

Ricardo Lozano was born and raised on a ranch outside Ojinaga and came to live in town in the 1990s. He began by playing the guitar but now says his primary instrument is the bajo sexto. "I always liked the music, the norteño music, I always intended to play it so I began playing when I was thirty," he said.

Juan Dominguez began playing music at the age of twelve. His father had a musical group while they lived on La Morita Ranch in Coahuila, Mexico. "My father looked at me and got the accordion and taught me," he said. In addition to his income from music, he also sells masa for making tamales. Before

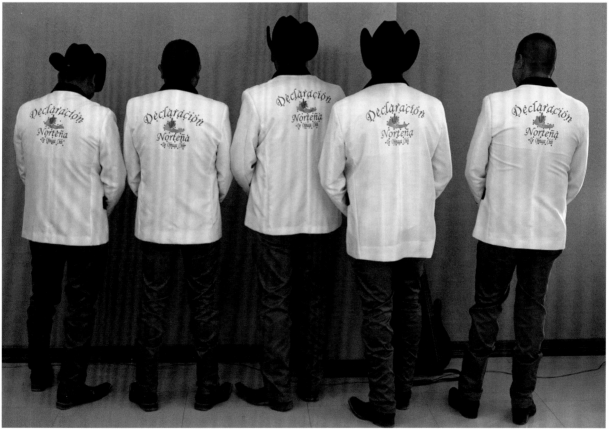

Declaración Norteño de Ojinaga. *Left to right*: Raymundo Sanchez, Ricardo Lozano, Juan Dominguez, Everardo Velazquez, and Lino Soto.

he joined Declaración Norteña, he was a member of Bravos de Ojinaga.

Everardo Velazquez was invited to be part of Declaración Norteña. "I was born in Ojinaga and stayed close by here in Val Verde, a ranch really close to Ojinaga," he said. He was invited to be their lead singer. He works in agriculture in addition to his work with the group.

Lino Soto was born in Ojinaga and his entire family lives there. He has been with the group less than a year. "They needed an accordion. I started with the guitar at ten, then started on the accordion at fourteen," he said. Lino's father was a musician who began teaching him to play the instruments. Lino is one of the few musicians who can make a living solely through his music.

When asked whether the Ojinaga Sound is as popular as norteño and Tejano, Lino said, "It depends on the people. I think it is as famous as the others. Each state will have their own type of norteño and there are a lot of differences between each state, especially here in Ojinaga."

Conjunto Primavera is one of the first bands that created the Ojinaga Sound, and most Ojinaga musicians agree it was in the late 1950s through the 1960s that this new style of norteño became popular.

Samuel Aguillera was born and raised in Ojinaga. He comes from a family of musicians active since 1945; his primary instrument is the accordion. Although his father did not want him to be a musician, Samuel started his music career at the age of nineteen. Samuel also makes a living as an HVAC technician in Ojinaga. He is the only member of the group Maximo Norte who lives in Ojinaga. He tours the United States, particularly in California, Georgia, Tennessee, Texas, Oklahoma, and Colorado. "I was invited to join the group because the owner is a singer and he was raised in Ojinaga but lived in Odessa and thought that something was missing. I am like the director of the group and I add that sound of Ojinaga to be able to sound like here," Samuel said. "Even in

Odessa when they hear the name Ojinaga, they know when they go, they will hear the Ojinaga Sound. Even if these groups are not living here, they probably have one member from Ojinaga, so they will say they are from Ojinaga."

Samuel explains the sound further as being more improvisational; although the saxophone and accordion are included in the characteristic music of other states in Mexico, it is different in Ojinaga. "We play a lot with the notes here, that's why the sound will be very different. They will interchange, up and down, up and down. Over there they just follow a line. We do more because of how we're listening to the music, not because of just reading the notes, more by ear," he said.

Julio Ramirez Reyes, the son of Julio Ramirez, who played the accordion for us at our first interview session in Ojinaga, is in the group La Leyenda del Bravo de Ojinaga. The other members are Aaron Mora, Francisco Ramírez, Martín Mata, and Efraín Luján. Julio began playing the accordion, following in his father's footsteps at the age of eleven. The group has been together for eleven years and tours mostly in Mexico while trying to renew visas to perform in the United States. "I started listening to my dad's group Los Guerrilleros de Chihuahua, Los Rebeldes del Bravo, and Conjunto Primavera," he said.

Julio has been able to make a living from his music, raising a family and sending his children to college. In addition to the accordion, Julio plays the drums, bajo sexto, and electric bass. He has seen a change in the sound since he was young. "When the norteño music first started, it was a little bit of another style, more a Monterrey style, they use the sax and accordion, but it will be very smooth. Then at some point the style changed for the accordion and saxophone. That is what makes it different here in Ojinaga. The people recognize the sound because it is different," he said. Julio also observed that in Chihuahua, their sound is very close to the Ojinaga Sound. Many groups identify themselves as being from Ojinaga but are not, and the sound is noticeably different.

Julio Ramirez Reyes of La Leyenda del Bravo de Ojinaga (*right*) and his father, Julio Ramirez.

Edgar Ivan Medrano (*left*) and Estanislao Medrano from Arrieros de Ojinaga.

His favorite instrument is the electric bass, and he likes to perform very romantic songs, playing original Mexican music but in a more romantic style. The song that the group is most often requested to play is "Corrido de los Mendoza," which they play at quinceañeras, weddings, and other events. The group also plays country music norteño. Julio likes to listen to Los Bukis, a group founded by Marco Antonio Solís, who plays older, original music in a romantic style. "We're doing a lot of songs from Juan Gabriel and Marco Antonio, putting norteño style to that," Julio said.

Mauricio Guerrero has been a member of the group Sangre Norteña de Ojinaga Chihuahua for fifteen years. He was born and raised in Ojinaga but left at the age of nineteen and went to the United States. The group tours in Dallas, Los Angeles, Nebraska, Oklahoma, and Denver. Every Thursday, Friday, and Saturday they travel and perform. He also works at the Presidencia, the municipal seat of Ojinaga.

The band plays "Adios, Adios Amor," a song that brings everyone to the dance floor. Mauricio finds that many bands name themselves for Ojinaga or make some reference to it, but they are not from there. "Because the older bands raised the name Ojinaga to the top of the style, every band wants to name themselves Ojinaga. Their parents may have been from here, but they were never raised here, but they all want to use the name. They don't have the same style norteño, it will not sound the same, and it will be too straight off the music, not real improvisation. Their music will be very calm," he said.

Estanislao Medrano has been a musician for twenty years and is in the group Arrieros de Ojinaga (Mule Drivers of Ojinaga). They have been together ten years and play in other states in Mexico. Estanislao was in another group before joining Arrieros de Ojinaga. He was raised in a musical family with relatives who sang. He was twenty-two when he first began playing the bass and makes his living from his music. He names "(Yo Tengo) La Ya Casita," a cumbia,

as the song that gets everyone dancing. The group plays mostly their own original music, and the song "El Viejo Café," also performed by Palito Ortega, made them popular.

Martin Velazquez Murillo is an accordion and saxophone player with Resplandor de Ojinaga Chihuahua, a group he founded in 1998. He is a career musician. When the group first began, they performed in the United States but now perform in Mexico because of problems obtaining visas. They have an active performing schedule, usually Friday, Saturday, and Sunday and frequently during the week.

Martin is a successful songwriter who also writes songs for other groups in Ojinaga. Some of his songs include "Dime Que No Te Irás" (Tell Me You Will Not Leave Me) and "Mirando las Estrellas," (Looking at the Stars). José Manuel Figueroa, among others, has influenced him. He is also in a group of songwriters. "We are a group that gets together and have, like, a platform. I send my songs and then they will send them to other groups, not only from Ojinaga, and they will buy them from there," he said. Martin also owns a recording studio.

Oscar Zuniga is a member of the group Conjunto Amanecer, which has been together for thirty-one years. He started with them because his father was their sound technician. He has played the drums for Conjunto Amanecer for five years. He also plays the bass and guitar.

Oscar was born in Coahuila, a state close to Chihuahua, but lives in Ojinaga now. He makes his living through his music, since the group is booked every weekend. They perform in the United States in Seattle, Denver, Miami, and California, among other locations. They do not have any problem with their older visas. "We have a special visa to go and work and play as a musician," he said. "It's mainly dances that we do over there."

Edwynn Madrid Lujan, another member of Conjunto Amanecer, began playing music at the age of twelve. He plays the electric bass, bajo sexto, ukulele,

Publicity photo from the early days of Conjunto Amanecer.

Grupo Amanecer (the original name of Conjunto Amanecer) with historic performance jackets. *Left to right*: Oscar Zuniga, Vico Madrid, Essary Madrid (now with Tierra Norteña), and Edwynn Madrid Lujan.

Stars in the sidewalk outside City Hall in Ojinaga, Mexico.

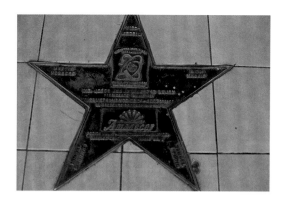

accordion, and guitar. Edwynn also sings with the group. He has been with them for five years.

His father, the oldest member of the group, taught elementary school on the ranches outside Ojinaga. "My dad started giving art classes, then bought an accordion and began playing it to the kids. That is how he started in music," Edwynn said. His father's friends heard he was playing the accordion, so they formed a group before Conjunto Amanecer. "That's how he and two of his friends got the Amanecer group started in 1985, from there they became very famous," Edwynn added. Conjunto Amanecer has a star outside City Hall. "The City Hall started to give a star to important people in Ojinaga and then they got one because of the thirty-two years they are the same group," Edwynn explained. Although the group began playing in Chihuahua, they are also known in the United States. They are asked to perform in the States at weddings, quinceañeras, and other events. "That's how the band got known in the US, because of the people that moved from Chihuahua or San Luis Potosí. The Mexicans that moved took the music with them," Edwynn said.

The five-member group has evolved from four families: Edwynn's three uncles, a brother, and the sons and cousins of the original members. Edwynn asks whether we would like to follow him to the tour bus, where they have the original suits from the beginning of the group. After a short drive, we see their tour bus and take pictures of the beautiful original performance suits. The group is obviously proud of their musical history in Ojinaga and beyond as one of the defining groups of the Ojinaga Sound.

Essary Madrid is in the group Tierra Norteña and is the son of the singer for Conjunto Amanecer. Essary was born in Chihuahua. "Back in those days

Mural at Ojinaga City Hall.

in Ojinaga, the health care was not very good, so the people would go and have their kids in the capital because of the hospital, then come back home," he said.

He began playing the bajo sexto in junior high at the age of fourteen and then started playing the accordion. He is currently a university student studying to be a music teacher. He played for three months with Conjunto Amanecer to help out, as many of the musicians in other groups do, even traveling on the same bus to perform. "The groups are very united. Different groups will go together to the main events they have in the same bus," he said. Essary will fill in for the group, singing and playing the bajo sexto when needed. His father and four of his brothers began Conjunto Amanecer, and the fifth brother plays in another group. The youngest member is a singer who is in the sixth grade.

The youngest musicians interviewed were Omar Marupo, sixteen, and Alfonso Matta, seventeen, who are the band Alto Nivel. They perform nearly every weekend and both play bass guitar. They have departed from the classic Ojinaga Sound. "We wanted to make something different because there's too many norteño groups. We wanted to create something different," said Omar. Their gigs are mostly parties and restaurants or bars in Ojinaga. Although they are creating a new sound, their favorite song to play is the same cumbia that Estanislao Medrano named as his favorite, "(Yo Tengo) La Ya Casita." Even though they are still in high school, the group has grown to four members.

As we spoke to these musicians and listened to their stories, their pride in their music and their love for performing became very clear. The Ojinaga Sound is certainly alive and well, and the musical tradition in Ojinaga is already continuing into the next generation.

3

A Tejano Legend
Sunny Ozuna

THE LEGENDARY SUNNY OZUNA of Sunny and the Sunliners is not a tall man, but he has a towering and magnetic stage presence. He appeared at the Agave Festival in Marfa, Texas, on June 8, 2018, the occasion of this interview. He is a familiar and welcome face in the Big Bend, since many people remember their grandparents and parents going to dances where he performed. Sunny Ozuna has toured the Big Bend, as have other well-known performers such as Little Joe Y La Familia and Ruben Ramos. When Ozuna's crossover hit "Talk to Me" landed on the Billboard national chart at number 11 in 1963, Ozuna and his Sunliners became the first Tejano musicians to be on the national chart (Los Tigres del Norte were number 1 in 1964 on the Latin Billboard chart). Sunny and the Sunliners were also the first all-Tejano band ever to appear on *Dick Clark's American Bandstand* in 1963. When he brought his style of Tejano music to the Big Bend, where norteño music was the most popular music from Mexico, his crossover hit drew cross-generational Mexican, Mexican American, and Anglo audiences. "Talk to Me," heavily played on radios across the country, was a bridge between Tejano and mainstream pop music.

The Big Bend is a special place to Sunny. This particular stretch of the US-Mexico border is home to a wide variety of binational music and blends of norteño and conjunto, but he brought a new hybrid to the music of the region, already known for the unique Ojinaga Sound. "The Big Bend was very important to us because we wanted to visit the people there to introduce the blend of Tejano music and English music. We knew we had a lot of fans and music lovers there that simply love to dance," he said. Decades later, with sixty-nine productions on the market, Sunny still regards the Big Bend as important to him. "We anxiously await our next visit to the Big Bend," he said.

Born Ildefonso Fraga Ozuna on September 8, 1943, in San Antonio, Texas, Sunny grew up listening to rock and roll and R&B, including doo-wop groups and Motown, in the 1950s and 1960s. "We were like all the kids of our time, killing ourselves to get to the TV set to see *Dick Clark's American Bandstand*," Sunny said. In 1957 and 1958, Sunny and Rudy Guerra formed a group named Sunny and the Sunglows with six other teenage members. The original members were Sunny on vocals, George Strickland on drums, Al Conde on guitar, Perry Norwood on bass, and Rudy Guerra on

Sunny Ozuna.

Sunny still brings the crowds to their feet.

saxophone. Sunny and the Sunglows were high school students at Burbank High School in San Antonio, playing gigs at churches, school dances, and talent shows. They became well known in San Antonio and surrounding towns.

Sunny was the only musician in his family. "I was kind of an oddball, but I really liked it. I don't know why. But I felt it in my heart, from day one, that [music] was going to be something that I would be doing for a pretty long time," he said. Besides being an accomplished vocalist, he is also an instrumentalist. "I really enjoy playing guitar and since I also became a songwriter, it came in handy. I wrote many of our hits that we recorded along the way through the years, a lot

of the songs that became big hits for us," he said. "After a while, we found that the songs I was writing would actually help to extend our success in the business."

As their popularity grew, the young group realized they needed a direction. The first song Sunny ever wrote was titled "Just a Moment," and it helped launch them, leading to gigs in small towns outside San Antonio. "We worked all the little towns around San Antonio but we couldn't go too far, because we were teenagers in high school. Our Hispanic parents always insisted, 'Let me see that diploma first, then you can do whatever you want.' I knew that I had to finish high school before I could get in full swing of a career," Sunny laughed.

In 1962 Sunny and the Sunglows recorded the song "Golly Gee" for the Okeh recording label, which also picked up the song for national distribution. But the song they first recorded in 1963, "Talk to Me," for Manuel Guerra of Sunglow Records, a cover of Little Willie John's song written by Joe Seneca, became their first major hit and launched their careers. When Sunny was a senior in high school, he was asked to appear with the Sunglows on *Dick Clark's American Bandstand* in Philadelphia. His dream was becoming a reality.

At a performance in Houston, record producer Huey P. Meaux heard "Talk to Me" and brought the song to national attention. Top 40 radio stations made the song a big success, and on the 1963 Billboard charts it reached number 4 on the adult contemporary chart, number 12 on the R&B singles chart, and number 11 on the Billboard top 100, the first mainstream chart success for a Tejano band.

"God is good. My luck was that by the time I got to my senior year, never thinking that the song that was going to be my signature song, it would be in my hands in the year 1963," he said.

Their drummer at the time, Manuel Guerra, became the manager of the group and began guiding the young band in their next direction. "His idea of changing Spanish lyrics to the songs we were already playing in English didn't go over too well with the guys in the band," Sunny said. "The language we were speaking at home was very limited. We were not speaking Spanish correctly. They laughed and called it Tex-Mex. This idea of Manuel's led to the creation of a new genre of music called Tejano music," Sunny explained.

At first, this music did not have a name but was called Tex-Mex or Chicano music. The term "Tejano" did not arise until later. "It had its own unique sound, and we wanted it to be identified with the state of Texas. The sound reflects how people feel. This genre has been accepted by Hispanics across the nation as being the sentiments and culture of Texas everywhere," Sunny said.

Sunny Ozuna and the Sunliners at the Agave Festival, Marfa, Texas.

They improvised on their unique sound, which was a mix of rock and roll and R&B, blending with Spanish lyrics and adding different instruments as they went on to perfect the sound. "We were one of the first to carry the electric organ to the gigs, then added congas, trombones, and electric violins, just to improve on what we were doing," Sunny said.

Sunny, with the renamed Sunliners, left the Sunglows to branch out in his career, and many more hits and recordings followed as he spent over fifty years in the business. In June 2014 Sunny and the Sunliners performed in El Paso as part of "The Ultimate Old School Jam," including acts that baby boomers grew up with such as Gene Chandler, the Chi-Lites, Yvonne Elliman, and Deniece Williams, among others. I was at that show in the Don Haskins Center with the nearly sold-out crowd. All the acts were warmly received, but when a man strolled onstage wearing a white suit, turquoise shirt, and white panama hat, the entire audience rose to their feet, nearly drowning out the announcer

introducing Sunny Ozuna. Elderly women with walkers, middle-aged women, and young women alike were all screaming. It was the first time I had witnessed such cross-generational recognition of a performer.

I asked Sunny what he thought of all the people who claim "Talk to Me" as their song and how many met and fell in love to his music. "People come up to me all the time and tell me exactly that. They would say, 'You know what? I met this lady here and I married her thirty-five, forty years ago, because of you, man.' 'We went to one of your dances where I invited her, we now have five children and they all know about your music,'" Sunny said. "We've been through generations of friends and fans in my career. The parents have played our music in their homes and parties."

"Talk to Me" is not their only signature song. "Put Me in Jail," "Smile Now, Cry Later," "Golly Gee," "Please Mr. Sandman," "The One That's Hurting Is You," and "Think It Over" also identify the group. "Our signature songs have become so, so many. These songs have helped us to stay alive in the business one more year," Sunny said.

Sunny received a new opportunity when his good friend Freddie Martinez Sr., who owns Freddie Records, asked Sunny to participate in a CD featuring some of the "old school" artists. Ozuna, with Augustin Ramirez, Carlos Guzmán, and Freddie Martinez, performed as The Legends. "Maybe we will win a Grammy for the project," Freddie said. "We had a good laugh and said 'Yeah, right!'" Sunny remembers.

They did win at the Forty-Third Annual Grammy Awards in 2000 for Best Tejano Album with *¿Qué Es Música Tejana?* "The write-up in the headline in the *Los Angeles Times* was 'Grammy Awards Won This Year by Old Favorites.' We were so surprised that year that all the new, top artists of that year did not win the awards. All the awards were given to [longtime] people in the business like ourselves. The artists that were predicted to win were sitting in the front rows and the 'old favorites' were sitting behind them picking up all the awards," Sunny said.

Sunny tours most of the year to sold-out crowds in shows on Carnival Cruise Lines, works with The Legends, and plays old school R&B shows on the West Coast with the Sunliners. The current Sunliners backing Sunny are David "Sunny" Ozuna, drummer; Joe Revelez, keyboard; Rick Munoz, bass; Hector Molina, guitar; James Morales, trumpet; William Cervantes, trumpet; Rudy Mejia, trombone; and Jimmy Alaniz, saxophone. In addition to performing with the Sunliners and The Legends, Sunny travels as a solo artist. He also performs occasionally with other groups. His awards are far too numerous to list, and he has over eighty-five different productions on the market. Sunny records on his own Key-Loc Records, managed by his son David S. Ozuna.

Sunny was inducted into the Texas Music Hall of Fame in 2000, and an anthology CD titled *Mr. Brown Eyed Soul* was released by Big Crown Records of New York in 2017.

It is nearly time for the show in Marfa. All the seats are filled and Sunny's opening act is the Resonators, featuring Molly Ferguson, the 2017 Tejano Idol Award winner. The lights dim and Sunny strolls onstage, clearly delighted to be here. The fans rise to their feet to welcome a Tejano legend.

4

The Venues

THE MUSICAL VENUES IN the Big Bend are a mix of older, established bars with dance floors and spaces that also accommodate special events such as weddings and large audiences. Private ranches also serve as venues for events and parties. We interviewed owners, former owners, and musicians who remember the historical sites.

There are music festivals throughout the year in the region. Viva Big Bend is an annual summer event with over fifty bands performing. The festival has been host to such well-known acts as Little Joe, the Texas Tornados, Ruben Ramos, and Los Lonely Boys. The festival begins at the Starlight Theatre in Terlingua and then continues in Marfa, Fort Davis, and Marathon.

In April 2019, Terlingua hosted the first Sotol Fest, a celebration built around a spirit similar to tequila and mescal that is distilled from the sotol plant native to northern Mexico. The weekend begins at La Kiva, featuring sotol, master distillers from Mexico, and local musicians. The next day there is a caravan to Boquillas, Mexico, where according to the website, "a celebration of unity + peace + dignity and respect" takes place. Back in Terlingua on Saturday night, the party continues with Mike and the Moonpies, local bands the Doodlin' Hogwallops, Los Pinche Gringos, and Scott Walker.

The Trans-Pecos Festival of Music + Love takes place at El Cosmico campground in Marfa. It is a weekend full of activities including live music performances. Marfa's Agave Festival in August has a full schedule of authors, tastings, and live music performances. In 2018, Sunny and the Sunliners were the headliners for the festival.

The Alpine Artwalk in November, now in its twenty-sixth year, promotes the arts and artists of the area, featuring live music in several areas throughout Alpine. The proceeds from the walk go to arts programs in the schools and promote art in the area.

Marfa Army Air Field

In December 1942 the first class of cadets arrived for flight training at the new Marfa Army Air Field. They earned their wings in February 1943, and a new class completed training each month until May 1945. This provided an opportunity for the musicians of the area to perform at dances and events each weekend,

Eduardo Alvarez, in his nineties, recalls playing in pickup bands in the Big Bend in the 1940s.

including chances to sit in with bands from outside the area, some of whom needed local musicians to perform with them.

The oldest musician we interviewed was Eduardo Alvarez, in his midnineties, who lives in Balmorhea, Texas. He was a teenager at the time the air field was open and is typical of musicians who performed with the bands in the area: pickup bands, groups assembled based on the instruments played and availability for these gigs. Although some musicians played at the air field, Eduardo did not, because he joined the army in 1944. The air field brought in bands from outside, but the musicians of the Big Bend who did play at the base became very skilled in playing the big band music of that era.

Eduardo continued to perform with other groups. "It wasn't really a band. It was another guy that was gifted, he was really good at the fiddle, and we used to play with him. Somebody told him I played the guitar. I didn't know how to play too good at that point. I just taught myself. He wanted to play with me and he thought I was good enough to play at the dances too. So I started to play with him and we played for a long time," Eduardo said. They played in Alpine, Marfa, Fort Davis, and Balmorhea.

He also played with an orchestra for an event when the guitar player was too ill to perform. "Somebody told the leader that I played the guitar. I had a filling station there, so he came and asked if I could play. 'They tell me you play the guitar? I couldn't get my guitar player to come over. You think you could play with us?' I said, 'I don't think so. I've never played with an orchestra.' He said, 'Let me be the judge.' After I played for him, I played with the orchestra," Eduardo said.

One of Eduardo's favorite songs was "Jesusita en Chihuahua," which he performed that night. For that evening's work, he earned twenty-five dollars, which at the time was a month's salary. The average pay for a gig was eight dollars for each musician, which was a week's pay.

Eduardo brought out his guitar, which was missing some strings. He had not played for many years. "I never play this one. The strings are not even on there. It's been a long time. I have an electric guitar with an amplifier. My son gave me the amplifier. I can't move my fingers. I got arthritis," he said.

The Jukebox in Lajitas

Bill Ivey grew up in Lajitas, where his father owned the iconic Trading Post. Bill owns the Trading Company and the Starlight Theatre in Terlingua. There were nickelodeons at the Lajitas Trading Post that were powered by a generator since there was no electricity in Lajitas. When a jukebox was added, Bill's job as a teenager was to stock it with records. "I came across a bunch of old seventy-eight rpm records that were in the nickelodeons, and some of them were very familiar and they're still performing those old songs today. I learned from buying music to put on my jukebox," Bill said.

Bill Ivey stocked his father's jukebox at the Trading Post in Lajitas as a teenager.

Bill had always loved the music that came out of San Antonio, such as Little Joe Y La Familia and Sunny Ozuna, but no one played that music in the jukebox. "I tried some more Latino music, but it wasn't played either. There were certain records that were literally worn out. Vicente Fernandez records, the Coyotes de Ojinaga, Conjunto Primavera, who became superstars and had kinfolk in the area. This was before they were superstars, but how they got their start is that they would come across that dirt road from San Carlos, sneak into the United States to go play a wedding or something, but they always stopped at the Trading Post. And they would play a dance to have enough gas money to get going," Bill said. "They would play on the porch and just pass the hat for money."

Bill had difficulty finding 45s in Spanish, so he made trips to El Paso and crossed into Juárez to find records for the jukebox. "It scared me in a way when I realized I was responsible for [my customers'] taste in music. It dawned on me that my family really and truly developed their taste in music because that was the only music," he said.

Juan Gabriel and Pedro Infante were popular with the older people in the area. The young people could hear the radio station in Ojinaga at night with transistor radios, but without electricity there was no exposure to more contemporary music such as rock and roll from radio stations elsewhere in Texas, except through records and, later, when Wolfman Jack became popular with teenagers on both sides of the border.

Bill realized that the music that was most popular in Lajitas was the music people grew up with; it was familiar. Business employees came from San Carlos, Mexico, worked, and then crossed back into Mexico at Paso Lajitas. The area developed into one community from two countries. "It took me a long time to really realize it, but [the jukebox] served all of the communities in Mexico and the communities on this side and became neutral territory," Bill said. Dances drew people from both sides of the border.

The music scene has changed dramatically in Terlingua. "Everybody's got an iPhone now, they've got Amazon music or iTunes. They are exposed to so much more music, different types of music that they now develop their own taste in music, whereas before, they couldn't," Bill said.

Terlingua

Terlingua, like Marfa, has a mystique all its own. It had the reputation of being where old hippies and fiercely independent outliers went to live. It is true that the residents of Terlingua, only fifty-eight in 2010, were committed to living off the grid if they chose, being completely self-sufficient. Others used generators for electricity and installed indoor plumbing. The scarcity of housing made it necessary to build their own homes. The population of Terlingua according to 2017 population figures is eighty, with a median household income of $94,750 and a median age of sixty-nine.

In the 1970s, the first wave of residents from outside the area came to live in Terlingua. It is a far different place now, with internet service, television and cell service, municipal water service, and a large emergency medical service center. When Big Bend High School opened in 1997, residents no longer had to send their children to Alpine, nearly two hours away. But not all these changes have been welcome to longtime residents, accustomed to informally gathering at their neighbors' homes for food, visiting, and music for entertainment.

Terlingua is a popular stopover for tourists visiting the 800,000-acre Big Bend National Park for camping, hiking, and river raft tours. Tourism is a mainstay of the economy.

Paso Lajitas, just twelve miles away, was an informal port of entry to Mexico and the United States but was closed after 9/11. As a result, restaurants and businesses closed on both sides of the border. Lajitas is home to the Lajitas Golf Resort. Austin businessman Steve Smith bought the town and twenty-five thousand additional acres at auction in 2000 to build a luxurious resort. In 2007 investors bought the property after Smith's money ran out. It is more affordable now and even attracts tourists to Big Bend National Park.

Although Terlingua accommodates tourists, the opportunity to easily visit the Mexican side of the Rio Grande is severely limited. Permanent residents of Terlingua feel the effects of small towns across the border becoming ghost towns. Previously those residents regularly crossed the Rio Grande to work and shop; that is mostly impossible now.

Two events that attract thousands of visitors are the fifty-two-year-old Tolbert-Fowler Cookoff and the CASI (Chili Appreciation Society International) Chili Cookoff. Both events take place on the same weekend in November. Originally named the Terlingua Chili Cookoff in 1967, the event started as a challenge when H. Allen Smith, author and New York humorist, challenged Wick Fowler, owner of the chili company Wick Fowler's Two-Alarm Chili, claiming no one in Texas could make real chili. The first contest drew 250 people and ended in a draw. The number of people coming to the original cookoff increased dramatically, but over the years when attendance dwindled, the CASI joined in on the November weekend, and attendance grew again.

Now there are Airbnbs, motels, and vacation rentals in Terlingua to accommodate tourist season. The restaurants attract residents in the other towns in the Big Bend as well as tourists. Terlingua is far from being gentrified, however, and still has the reputation of being remote, even by Big Bend standards.

Voices from Both Sides

This annual event, established in 2013, was the brainchild of Collie Ryan and Jeff Haislip of Terlingua. It now draws hundreds of people to the tiny communities of Paso Lajitas near Terlingua and Lajitas and San Carlos, Mexico. More than a gathering of musicians and citizens of both sides of the border, it is also

an international protest over the border closure. Ryan and Haislip decided that a party would be more fitting, a "fiesta protesta." The event also demonstrates what was lost when the small communities along the Rio Grande were separated when the border closed. Paso Lajitas, Mexico, depended on tourism. Lajitas was a substation port of entry into Mexico and provided easy access for both sides to shop, visit family, go to the doctor, and work on the US side on ranches and in businesses in Terlingua. Schoolchildren crossed the river to attend school in Terlingua. Since the border closure, the residents of Paso Lajitas have dwindled to only a few families, and the restaurants are closed. Residents of the small community of Lajitas, on the US side, in addition to Terlingua have lost their customers from Mexico. Now, families in San Carlos, Mexico, see their families across the river only once a year, although they live only sixteen miles from the border. The nearest legal port of entry is at Boquillas, which is frequently closed, or at Ojinaga, both over an hour away.

The event that inspired the protest happened in 2012 on Mother's Day weekend. Laird Considine remembers that day. "We also call it Black Friday. It was a raid that happened, because after they shut down the border, everyone kind of fled because no one knew what was going to happen after 9/11. But nothing seemed to happen so they started to kind of drift back in. Then, it was May 10, 2002, that they came with paddy wagons, helicopters . . . it was a huge scene. They went and arrested the boat guy. He was sixteen years old. He was rowing people across the river down at Lajitas."

Mark Lewis was not in Terlingua at the time but has heard from his friends of the impact of the raid. "All of a sudden down here families disappeared out of their houses overnight and were never able to come back again because they didn't have the papers. I've heard about it through my friend, who was the trauma therapist counselor for the whole Big Bend, how traumatic it was for this community to just have its heart ripped out."

Laird Considine
remembers the
immigration raids of
May 2012 that helped
instigate Voices from
Both Sides.

In the effort to shut down the border, the communities on both sides were nearly paralyzed. Crossing the river to work on the US side was an everyday occurrence; children crossed to go to school—and then everything changed. "I was working in Lajitas, and workers were just dropping their tools and running for the border, and the helicopters were swooping down. They arrested . . . I don't know how many people they loaded up and hauled away. And then they came around to the communities and started going door to door," said Laird. Everyone who could come back legally figured out a way to return, and those who could not relocated elsewhere in the state of Chihuahua or, to stay in the area, moved to Ojinaga.

Prior to the Voices from Both Sides event, the National Park Service sponsored a "Good Neighbor Day" that hosted people from both sides of the border and included music and cultural dancers from Mexico. "That was fun to play every year and see all the people from other communities—from Boquillas, and from San Vicente, and from San Carlos, and cool kids coming in from as far away as Pecos and Presidio to put on their dances. After 9/11 we quit being good neighbors and that event got shut down. But that was a similar kind of party," said Laird.

Mark Lewis has been the director of music for Voices from Both Sides for the past several years. He coordinates the schedule. The leaders of Paso Lajitas and San Carlos, Mexico, joined in the organization of the event. "It's the happiest party I've ever seen. It's a labor of love for me," Lewis said.

As the music coordinator for the event, Mark has concentrated on the local musicians. "The people who are on the road chasing stardom are there in the Starlight, but at Voices from Both Sides, the people I put up on the stage there aren't the people from Austin who want to be on that stage. They call me and they ask, and I say I'm sorry. This is old-time locals and young old-time locals, and those who are maybe getting a good start on becoming an old-time local. And that's my priority," he said. Carlos Maxwell headlined in 2017.

The event was covered in *Texas Monthly* and the *New York Times* and was featured on the Samantha Bee television show *Full Frontal*. "I thought they did a pretty good job of capturing the absurdity of the fact that the border is closed through this area and this party that happens every year. First year it happened, no one knew what was going to happen really. Didn't know if Border Patrol was going to get involved, if it was going to be okay," said Laird. At first it was a small gathering on both sides, but there were more people on the Mexico side of the river, where they set up tents, chairs, tables, and food. "On the American side there were a bunch of people like me, Dr. Fun, and Charlie all sitting on rocks in the full sun with acoustic guitars in our hands. Someone came up to me and said, 'Now, if you were just walking here and you didn't know anything, which one of these countries would be the third world country?' We're all literally sitting on the dirt. We have no shade, no generator, no stage," said Laird. The bands on the Mexico side of the river were wearing performance clothes and had shade and tents and a large audience. "We're just sitting on rocks with our guitars. We had some instruments with us and a cheesy little generator. Ted wandered across the river and started talking to those guys. He hollered on their microphone, 'Hey! Pinche Gringos, come on over. They want us to play!' So we all waded the river and started playing on their side," he said.

The increase in popularity of Voices from Both Sides not only draws people from far away but also is important to this small community. For many people, it is their annual opportunity to see aunts, uncles, cousins, and other family members who cannot cross over to the US side of the border. For this one day they meet in the middle of the Rio Grande to see one another. Generations of residents on both sides were formerly connected—not separated—by a river that was not a barrier. The event is an affirmation that they are still one community, despite the closed border.

Laird has been a part of the tightly knit river guides and has found that the division between the

Mark Lewis directs Voices from Both Sides.

Mike Davidson promotes the Texas River Music series, featuring trips
down the Rio Grande in the company of Texas singer-songwriters.

two countries can be nearly invisible. "The river guiding community is out there every day on this so-called border, people come here and they walk up to the edge of the river and they go, 'That's Mexico.' When you're out there every day, you lose all track of thinking that's Mexico over there and this is America over here. It's one big, beautiful river going through this awesome ecosystem and geology and history and culture. It seems so artificial, especially when you're just out there in the boat and you're spending the night camped out on either side," he said.

Residents of both sides of the border frequently help one another when needed. Laird spent two hours with another guide helping to dig a cow out of the mud. "These guys showed up in a pickup truck, because we weren't getting anywhere. They had ropes and we helped them. We're in the river up to our thighs in the muck and we helped get those ropes around this poor calf that was stuck in the mud. They tied it to the bumper of the truck. We're all heaving and we finally get the cow out of it. The mama cow is all happy and the Mexicans are all happy. We're all happy. You know, it's just a tiny little incident of a billion of them that happen all the time here," he said.

Every year, Voices from Both Sides reunites a divided community and demonstrates to the visitors who attend the event that these two countries are one community. Mark Lewis said, "When we go down and do Voices from Both Sides, it's a neighborhood picnic for a community with a broken heart. Every single one."

Texas River Music Series

Far Flung Adventures, which had its beginnings in 1977, features guided river rafting trips, hikes, and tours. The enterprise also offers the Texas River Music series, started in 1983 as a three-day rafting trip featuring gourmet meals and evening performances by well-known musicians such as Joe Ely, Jerry Jeff Walker, Jimmie Dale Gilmore, Butch Hancock, and

others over the years. "We did our first music river trip with a guy named Bobby Bridger. There was a person on that trip who knew Steven Fromholz and made the introduction. That would've been 1984 or 1985," Mike Davidson said. A radio personality in Austin and his wife, a music promoter, contacted Mike. "Shortly thereafter we promoted a river trip with Butch Hancock. Just like Steve Fromholz, Butch became enamored with the desert and with running the river," he said. Butch built his home in Terlingua and stayed. Mike quit the river rafting aspect of the business in 2001, when they would have done the last music trip. "We began reviving this concept last year, did two successful trips this October, and are encouraged to plan four dates for fall 2020," Mike said.

Butch Hancock is a member of the roots band the Flatlanders. A Texas River Music reunion trip in the 1990s with Jimmie Dale Gilmore, Joe Ely, and Butch led to touring and performing again several years later. Butch, a well-respected musician living in Terlingua, maintains an extensive touring schedule.

The Musicians on the Porch at Terlingua

The Terlingua Trading Company, originally the company store of the Chisos Mining Company, is located in the Terlingua Ghost Town. Rex Ivey operated the Trading Post, and his son Bill Ivey and his family have maintained the family tradition. The Porch has an iconic status as the place musicians gather informally in Terlingua. There are guitars on the Porch for anyone to play, and throughout the day residents and tourists stop awhile to drink beer, relax, and listen as the musicians jam.

We met Charles "Carlos" Maxwell, fiddler Mark Lewis, Laird Considine of Los Pinche Gringos, and guitarist Dr. Fun on the storied front porch of the Terlingua Trading Company, where they had gathered to tell their stories.

Carlos Maxwell was born in Monahans, Texas. He came from a musical family; his mother played

Pickers on the porch at Terlingua. *Left to right*: Carlos Maxwell, Mark Lewis, Dr. Fun, Laird Considine.

Carlos Maxwell.

keyboards and sang, his father played mouth harps, and his sister played keyboards and accordion and also sang. "From early on, I was involved in gospel music and country music. I got my first guitar when I was about seven years old. My mother also played guitar. She taught me a few chords on the guitar, so I was exposed to music most of my life, but I didn't start my performing career until 1973," Carlos said.

He had been to Terlingua many times over the years, since he was raised in West and South Texas. He came to live in Fort Davis, but when he began touring he was based in New Orleans. "Then one day I woke up and said, 'It's time to go home,' so we came to Terlingua. That was 1978 or '79. Had a family,

children. We all came here and lived. I based my musical career after that point just in the Big Bend area pretty much. We didn't leave much to play other places. Occasionally El Paso or played in Austin a little bit, but basically, stayed in the Big Bend area," he said. Carlos played with the musicians in Terlingua, including a band called Chisos with Chris Müller and Jason Harvey. He played with Doug Davis for ten years. "Bill Pat McKinney was one of the first people I played with and we had a little honky-tonk band and played a lot around Terlingua Ranch. There was a store twenty miles up the road here and we played in that store a lot. A lot of the Saturday night dances. That was the time when people loved to dance and they would come out; anytime we'd strike a guitar they'd start dancing," Carlos said. He also played frequently with Craig Carter.

"A lot of us are kind of alumni of playing with the Spur of the Moment band. They put this idea together of doing this Mexican music. We put the Pinche Gringos together and it was kind of a breakthrough, I thought," Laird Considine said. If they were playing at La Kiva, they drew a Mexican audience. "They would be coming out and dancing and all the gringos were trying to watch the Mexicans and learning how to do the cumbias. After that border closure, it created not just that between us and what's just right over there, but culturally, people kind of retreated back into their little area," he added.

Carlos had a band from the Mexican side, and his children came from a ranch there to attend school in Terlingua. "All of a sudden the border is closed. And so they were asking, 'Where are we going to go to school? How are we going to do this? Where are we going to live?' There was a lot of shuffling that went on for a while there to keep life together," he said.

Mark Lewis was born and raised in Iowa, attended high school in Michigan, and went to college in Chicago. As a child, he studied classical music for ten years, but that did not ignite his passion for music. "It was after I got out of the whole classical thing and when I was in my late thirties. I didn't play anything for twenty years, from eighteen to thirty-eight. I started to learn to play the mandolin by ear and played as a street performer in Santa Barbara, California, every Saturday at the big farmers' market for years. I'd just drag anybody along and play any kind of tune that anybody brought," he said. He continued to do that for ten years and developed a five-member bluegrass band. They never practiced but became the most successful bluegrass band in Santa Barbara. Every Saturday they played at the farmers' market for dollar tips. "I did it for fun. I didn't do it for success because I was already getting old. So fun has always been the driver for me. Having fun, yeah. If I'm not [having fun], the fiddle's in the case and I'm on my way home. Pretty much the way I operate out here," Mark said.

He agrees with the other musicians that dances are becoming a thing of the past. Mark is a dance fiddler and plays square dances. "I've played forty, fifty dances on the West Coast around California and Portland. Square dancing is really popular, and people don't dance anymore, but there is a subculture of people hanging on to a square dance culture. And you can still get a bunch of old people out to two-step in Texas. There just aren't bands anymore. The singer-songwriter mentality is 'I'm performing and these are my songs,' and they generally perform without a band. It's certainly had an impact on any of that kind of thing happening here. That has become the musical subculture of the present," he said.

He came to Terlingua and worked as a river guide and farther west most of his adult life. When he arrived at the age of twenty-four, he was the lead instructor on a thirty-day backcountry program through the Texas Department of Corrections Texas Youth Commission. The goal was to get troubled youth back to their homes. "I worked a month on, month off. I'm down here in the wintertime. Spring and fall in the Gila Wilderness in New Mexico, and then in the summertime we'd go to the San Juan Mountains in Colorado with these adjudicated youth. They were so motivated. I got a lot of stories. It wasn't always easy,

but that's when I got to the Big Bend and certainly fell in love with it. Then I came back as a river guide in '90," Mark said.

Mike Kasper, the guitarist known as Dr. Fun, has long platinum hair and was dressed in a cowboy hat, western vest, and jeans. He brought a new inlaid guitar that he proudly displayed to the other musicians. He was born in Houston and fell in love with music at a very early age. "My mama had an icehouse outside of Conroe, Texas. She had a Wurlitzer jukebox, and as a tiny child, five years old, I would stick my head in between the speakers, and I would listen to Johnny Horton's 'North to Alaska' and 'From a Jack to a Queen,'" he said. His mother bought him a B tone guitar and dressed him as a cowboy. His guitar was red and printed with cowboys and Indians. "She would take me into the honky-tonks and bars. People would look up and I'm standing there with my guitar in front of the jukebox. She goes, 'Y'all gotta watch this.' She would put a nickel in the jukebox and I would belt out, 'I'm in love. I'm all shook up.' Five years old, doing air guitar like a little monkey on a chain. Puts money in the jar. That's how it all sort of started," Dr. Fun said.

Growing up in the piney woods of East Texas, he developed a love for the outdoors. When he came to the Big Bend for the first time in the early 1970s he thought he had found the real Texas. "I made a vow to myself that if it ever goes belly up in the big city, this is where I'm going to come take a stand. So, in 1985 the oil field industry went belly up. I packed everything in my van, a hundred and twenty-five dollars, a PA system, all of my paintings. I was a commercial technical illustrator," he said.

His new life in the Big Bend began in Alpine. He didn't know anyone and decided to go to the Railroad Blues with a demo tape and offered to play for tips if the owners liked what they heard. They played the tape on the spot and asked the customers whether they liked what they heard. "I've got demo songs: Cat Stevens, Kenny Loggins, Shake Russell, my favorites. She turned it off and she goes: 'What do you think?'

Michael Kasper,
a.k.a. Dr. Fun.

They all clapped. In two weeks I had enough gigs for three months," he said.

Although he landed these gigs, he still had to live in his van. He spent his days in the city park to avoid being labeled as a vagrant by the police. "At night, I went back to the Sunday House hotel in my van with my dog and my Coleman stove for cooking dinner. If I needed ice, I'd go to the ice machine," Dr. Fun said.

He met fellow musician Mike Marks and they formed a duo and had steady work. Then Mike moved to Terlingua to be a boatman. Dr. Fun was then living in a motel on the edge of Alpine. One Sunday morning after a gig on Saturday night, Mike came to Dr. Fun's door and told him to pack; he was taking him to Terlingua to be a boatman. Dr. Fun was a raft guide for eighteen years.

He sees a strong influence from Mexico in the music that is popular in Terlingua. "You can't really be in this area as a 'gringo' very long before you realize that the Mexican people who live here in this area are some of the most gracious, loving, kind families. They will take you into their house and feed you their last tortillas. And the music that they celebrate with their families, you get a big quinceañera going, and you're looking at happy feet, happy music." he said.

His music life in Terlingua and the friends he has made through the music keep Dr. Fun there. "It is from the musical experiences with Mike, Laird, Charlie, Mark, Ted . . . I can't name the number of musicians that I've sat with and joined and played with. That's why I'm here. I've been here ever since. Someday I'm going to have to pinch myself and say, 'Vacation's over, boy. You need to go home.'"

Sunday afternoon at three o'clock finds musicians on the Porch. Performed every week, their music has evolved into border music. "After a couple of months, it grows into something that sounds pretty Mexican and pretty indigenous here. That kind of stuff bleeds over into songs that Laird will write. You listen to his recordings and you'll hear something distinctive in there that sounds like it could have come from across the border. There is that sort of cross-border pollination," Mark said.

The Starlight Theatre and Restaurant, Terlingua

Built in the 1930s during the days of quicksilver mining, the Chisos Movie Theater provided entertainment for the area. When the mining was gone, the theater was abandoned to the elements until Terlingua saw an increase in residents. The Ivey family now owns the Starlight. Although roofless, it became the location for open-air events such as parties, concerts, and dances. A new roof was added to the Starlight along with major exterior refurbishment, followed by interior renovation in 2010. The Starlight has a full schedule of music and entertainment and a restaurant and bar.

La Kiva Restaurant and Bar, Terlingua

La Kiva was built in the early 1980s by Gilbert Felts. This cave restaurant and bar with a prehistoric theme is a unique and popular spot that attracts tourists headed to Big Bend National Park or local music festivals. When Gilbert passed away, his nephew Glenn took over La Kiva. He made it a popular venue by regularly scheduling musicians to play and established a weekly open mike night. It became a very popular local hangout in Terlingua, thanks to Glenn's colorful personality. Glenn was considered a patron saint of the local musicians because of his commitment to scheduling gigs regularly. After he passed away in 2014, La Kiva was bought by Josie and John Holroyd. The Holroyds, originally from the United Kingdom, came to the United States in 1980. John was a biotech engineer. Typical of other residents, they came to Terlingua in 1981 and fell in love with the Big Bend. They also maintain a residence in Minnesota, close to their family.

The tradition of featuring live music has continued, and renovations and expansion of the kitchen have helped La Kiva maintain its popularity for tourists and residents alike.

The Starlight Theatre.

Inside the Starlight.

La Kiva.

Alpine

After a week or so in the Big Bend, whether exploring the park or spending time in the small communities, a trip to Alpine can seem like an excursion to the big city. The seat of Brewster County, Alpine reported a population of 6,065 in 2017. Alpine is a friendly town and most of the residents know one another. Home to Sul Ross State University and its student population of 2,249, the community certainly has more retailers, gas stations, grocery stores, and restaurants than towns thirty minutes away: Marfa's population is 1,772 and Fort Davis has 1,201 residents, but both lack many of the services Alpine offers. Alpine has the

hospital, doctors, attorneys, and dentists who serve the Big Bend. The other communities in the region have limited medical services. Retirees often find it easier to live in Alpine than in the smaller or more remote areas of the Big Bend.

On the other hand, Alpine is not exactly gentrified, at least by some standards. There is no Starbucks, no Costco or Sam's Club. You have to travel to Midland or El Paso to shop at such places, and you may also need to make a similar trek to receive specialized medical care if needed.

Since Alpine is a college town, there are more young people than elsewhere in the region. There is a livelier club and bar scene because of the students. Alpine sports two large chain hotels and several other hotels and motels to house large numbers of people attending graduations and other events at Sul Ross. And of course many tourists frequent Alpine as well.

Railroad Blues

Richard Fallon and RC Toler are the former owners of Railroad Blues, a well-known and long-standing venue in Alpine. RC was born and raised in Houston but has made Alpine his home for over thirty years. "Very few people are born and raised out here. Everybody comes out here and likes it and stays, or comes back. Well . . .

you work your way back. You leave but you don't forget it. Eventually, you find a way to come back. I was just trying to get out of Houston," he said. "I wanted to get as far away from Houston as I could and stay in Texas. I never even heard of Alpine, and I looked on the map, found it, and came out here and rented," he said. He was forty when he moved to Alpine.

Richard was living in Austin before he came to Alpine. "At the time, I was working at a hotel up in North Austin. I was the beverage manager and I was wearing suits every day and was really tired of it," he said. His father-in-law loved the Big Bend and kept encouraging Richard to come out and open a bar in Alpine. He came to visit, stayed in Alpine one night,

Richard Fallon and RC Toler.

and hiked the South Rim in August 1993. He also crossed over to Boquillas, Mexico, and came back across to Terlingua. "We went to La Kiva, which at that time the big cottonwoods were still growing and the Starlight was recently opened. There was nobody down there. Both bars were just gorgeous. I couldn't believe it. Then I was told during the tourist season they're really busy. I just really fell in love with it. It was just beautiful out here. I had a brand new baby at the time and asked my wife if she'd consider moving out here and see how that worked. She agreed. We put the house on the market and gave notice at work, and I moved here three months later. Moved here Christmas Eve of '93 and never looked back," Richard said.

Richard and RC met and decided to open a bar with live music in mind. They bought Railroad Blues, a one-room bar, from previous owner Rick May, who operated it for ten years. "There were two of us, so we could divide the responsibilities. And we put a lot of effort in it and remodeled it with bands in mind. We put in a stage, a sound booth, a back room with dining room, showers, couches, and a door directly off the stage where they could go. We had that in mind, catering to bringing music here," RC said.

Before they could open, they had to remodel, so they worked day and night to open on April 4, with the grand opening on April 13. "We'd take turns, one of us would go home and shower and shave and come back and the other one would go home and shower and shave. We bartended. We did this every night," said Richard. It was one week later that an earthquake hit Alpine.

"We were behind the bar and all of a sudden the building started shaking. Stuff started falling off that shelf in front of the bar. RC thought that the train derailed. I had this vision of this thing on its side knocking all the buildings down. We yelled at the people in the poolroom, 'There's a train derailed!' We all run out the front door and the place was shaking. It felt like forever but then it just stopped. And there's no train," he said.

"We came in with a bang," RC added.

RC decided immediately that T-shirts were needed to mark the event. He went to the print shop around the corner and bought up every blue T-shirt they had in stock, eighty-two dark blue ones. He and Chris Ritchey came up with a simple design. "It was a cartoon train bouncing up and down and the tracks. 'I survived the earthquake at the Railroad Blues.' We sold out the next night," he said.

"It was a great weekend. Everybody came and wanted to talk about where they were during the earthquake. The place was packed," added Richard.

The success of Railroad Blues continued because of the variety of music they booked: country-western, rock and roll, even heavy metal and reggae. They also booked many singers and musicians in bands that were all women or women-fronted, including Sisters Morales, who performed at Railroad Blues for years, and Pork, a three-woman band with Dana Lee Smith on guitar, Edith Casimir on drums, and Marty Hattman on bass. All three were vocalists. They performed a type of punk music. Patrice Pike was also a regular at Railroad Blues. Toni Price, a well-known singer from Austin, came to play and fell in love with the Big Bend. "She had a record deal with Antone Records for a live recording. She came out with an eighteen-wheeler with a studio in the front. The album was called *Soul Power* and was number one in Austin for several months," Richard said.

"The first band we had out was Percy Struthers. He's been in Minnesota forever, but he's real-deal blues. No pick: fingerpicking. Originally born in Meridian, Mississippi. He left home at thirteen. Reads like a typical blues story. They hung his dad in the front yard. His uncle taught him how to play the guitar. His mom gave him all the money she had hidden in the house, a bag full of clothes, the guitar, and told him to go north. And he listened. He ended up in Minnesota," RC said.

"The year he played our place he won the W. C. Handy Blues Award. That was the first big band and

Iconic fire truck and sign at the Railroad Blues.

then two weeks later we had Alejandro Escovedo play," said Richard. Alejandro told other musicians about his experience in Alpine, and Richard and RC began getting more calls for bookings.

"He went back and spread the word in Austin, so we had everybody that was anybody through the years from Austin. The people that like Austin like Alpine. There's chemistry there. And it goes both ways," said RC.

Over the years, Richard and RC have seen the music in the area change dramatically. When they first arrived, country and western dominated the music scene; there were no reggae or Tejano acts booked at the club. "There was a real void here for the Mexican citizens. They didn't really have a good club to go to. That's a void we filled. We had a lot of cowboy places here that didn't roll out the carpet for them," said RC.

"I think that the Mexican music is fun. It's danceable. I think it reaches across all cultures. When we had the Pinche Gringos here, people would hit the floor for the cumbias and it would be bikers, and cowboys, and the Hispanic population, and students, and teachers, and everything . . . *bam*! On the floor," Richard continued.

The Railroad Blues was wildly popular because RC and Richard were booking acts that varied from the steady diet of country and western that was played exclusively on the radio. "There was a desire for all kinds of music that wasn't being fulfilled out here. I think we just happened to fill that void at the right time because people came out. We could have anybody playing there and they would show up. They just wanted to hear something other than country.

And we had a lot of country and western, too. It goes over good," said RC.

Even during the era of rock and roll, the previous owners of the radio station did not vary the music from country and western. "Well, in those days it was like listening to the *Twilight Zone* music. Back in 1947 they bought a hundred albums. Maybe fifty. I'm not talking about the owner now, but the previous owner played pretty much the same music for the next fifty years," RC explained.

They owned Railroad Blues for nineteen years and during that time hosted the first Saint Patrick's Day event, which was disappointing because the keg of Guinness and the corned beef and cabbage proved to be not much of a draw. Richard believes it was because RC was the only Irishman out there. They also began a Cinco de Mayo event, also the first one ever. They have an antique fire truck parked outside the club, and with the addition of speakers brought from home and an amplifier from the club, they played music and started a parade that became an annual tradition. "We had a band from East Los Angeles called the Blazers that used to play for us all the time, from the same neighborhood as Los Lobos. They know them really well. They were on Rounder Records, which is just a real American roots label. They played East LA Chicano rock. They'd do cumbias and rock them up and they'd do rock and roll. During the Cinco de Mayo parade that's what we played every year. We played the Blazers' CDs. We packed it in for that," said Richard.

As the reputation of the club grew, they were able to book well-known performers. When band tours went west, instead of stopping overnight in El Paso, they began booking a night in Alpine. Little Joe Y La Familia performed regularly to standing-room-only crowds. Little Joe is also very popular with the older crowd. "We'd open at four o'clock. In come all these little old ladies that never go to bars. They go to church and they come home. Well, they would be there, grab all the seats; because usually it was such a crowd we'd take the tables out a lot of times. They would grab every barstool around. They're there at four o'clock. I thought, 'They're going to be wasted by six, because the show doesn't start until ten,'" RC laughed.

Jerry Jeff Walker also appeared at the club several times and was amazed at the intimacy of the venue, since he usually appeared in arenas and large theaters. He thoroughly enjoyed himself and became an admirer of Richard's sangria, a signature recipe of the club. Arlo Guthrie, Ray Wylie Hubbard, and Canned Heat also performed at Railroad Blues, among others. Richard and RC were booking acts five nights a week, unheard of in a town the size of Alpine nearly twenty years ago. They were also host to international bands through an organization that sponsors the performers in a sort of exchange program, which is how Railroad Blues hosted three Chinese bands. "Two did half English, half Chinese. The last band hung out at the café that was right off Tiananmen Square. They were a political rock band and performed in Chinese," Richard said. They also booked bands from Chile, Germany, and Africa. Richard remembers a band from Ireland. "They were called 'We Should Be Dead' from Limerick. Those girls looked like little leprechauns. They were amazing."

Richard and RC made the tough decision to retire and sell the club. They put the club on the map thanks to publicity in *Texas Monthly* and other publications that regularly listed it among the top clubs in Texas. They knew that it took a total commitment of time; one of them, at least, had to be there all the time. They also successfully retained their employees, some for over fifteen years. Since they started the club, Alpine has grown and more venues have opened. The new owner lives in El Paso and the club has changed. The once bright red fire truck has faded in the desert sun and lost its shine. The pool table is still there and music still plays on the sound system, but the innovative vision of Richard and RC during the early formative years of club music in Alpine is now a part of local history.

Harald Mois, proprietor of Harry's Tinaja, in Alpine.

Harry's Tinaja: Harald Mois

A tinaja is a depression or pocket in bedrock usually found below waterfalls or caused by spring flow or water from arroyos. To German Harald Mois, it seemed an appropriate name for a bar. Harald left Germany for his health because of lung problems. After living in French Polynesia on the Marquesas Islands for close to three years, he wanted to go to Guatemala and the Pacific coast. "I found a little place in America on the Mexican border. Came on Amtrak from Los Angeles. Got off in Alpine and loved it and stayed," Harry said. He has been in Alpine since 1999 and opened the bar in 2007. His bar is Alpine's answer to the Porch in Terlingua. There are guitars out in the bar that anyone is welcome to play. "My sign out there says, 'Pickers are welcome. All ages.' I have guitars. I have an accordion. I have washboards. I have a mandolin back there in the corner. I have a banjo at home. In good weather, people are outside playing music," he said.

Harry was a brewmaster in Germany and for ten years owned bars and restaurants. Harry's Tinaja is in a building that was once a car rental and U-Haul business and was also once the first cell phone store in Alpine.

He began buying equipment and transforming the space. "I had two months' time. You've got to put in the application, and if nobody complains, then you can have a bar. Nobody complained. You have sixty days to do everything you see right now, not the decorations, but all the outside and the bar," he said. The walls are covered with colorful nostalgic beer ads, and nearly everything is all about Texas.

Harry also has musicians passing through Alpine who perform at his bar, Alpine being a good overnight stopover for band and musician tours. His performance space is outside because the inside space is

Harry's Tinaja.

Harry and some of the regulars.

so limited. Harry was a regular customer at Railroad Blues when Richard Fallon and RC Toler were the owners. Harry believes that was the best music venue in Alpine.

He is seeing a change in the age of his clientele. "I consider myself to be the town bar. Everybody comes, from college professors to mayors to the church people. Come evening, the young kids are here. I don't deal so much with the college people. It's just too much stress," he said. "We have so many underage, and that was the reason I wanted a small space. I don't have liquor, just beer and wine. Just keep it calm and everybody comes. Like my T-shirt says, 'Everybody's welcome at least once,' which is how it is," Harry explained.

Musicians passing through Alpine get the opportunity to play their new tunes, gauging crowd reaction from a smaller audience before they appear in larger venues. Since Harry has never had a cover charge, it is an inexpensive way to spend an evening listening to live music.

The Ole Crystal Bar

The Ole Crystal Bar is a large space on Holland Avenue. New owners renovated the bar in 2016, installing pool tables, large TVs, shuffleboard, and a large dance floor with regular live music. Tuesdays are open mike nights. Indoor and outdoor dining are also offered. The inside seems familiar to most Texans,

The Ole Crystal Bar.

Ritchey Hotel.

RITCHEY HOTEL, 1886. FRAME AND ADOBE. BUILT FACING OLD CATTLE LOADING PENS ON THE SOUTHERN PACIFIC RAILWAY.

LODGINGS AND SALOON FOR COWHANDS AND RANCHERS IN TOWN TO SHIP CATTLE FROM WIDELY SCATTERED RANCHES OF THE BIG BEND COUNTRY.

RECORDED TEXAS HISTORIC LANDMARK-1965

since many bars with dance floors and live music share the same ambience. It is usually busy, even when there is no live music scheduled.

Ritchey Wine Saloon and Beer Garden

The Ritchey Wine Saloon and Beer Garden was originally the Hotel Ritchey when it opened in 1886; it remained a hotel until the early twentieth century. The location became a bar and restaurant in the 1950s. Located directly across from the Amtrak station, the Ritchey hosted railroaders on stopovers, and passengers would come in during scheduled stops.

It was closed for nearly fifty years until it reopened a year ago under new owners. The Ritchey has been renovated to reflect its historical significance to Alpine.

Musicians come in to play on Sundays, usually acoustic guitar, and larger groups usually appear on Thursday, Friday, or Saturday. The venue also features speakers and poets. It is a quiet place without televisions that attracts a steady stream of locals. Mark Hinshaw, the food and beverage manager, plans to oversee the addition of a new kitchen with an expanded menu.

The Holland Hotel

The restored historic Holland Hotel is a popular venue for local musicians and small musical groups. One evening, Michael Stevens invited Don Cadden, Todd Elrod, Matt Skinner, Neil Trammell, and Jim Wilson to join him in the lobby of the hotel for what he called a "pickin' session." All played acoustic guitar except Todd Elrod, who played harmonica. As they began to play in the lobby in front of the fireplace, people began crowding the space, coming from the hotel's Century Grill to hear the music. The crowd was entertained with songs such as "Tonight We Ride" by Tom Russell and

Informal picking session at the Holland Hotel. *Left to right*: Don Cadden, Todd Elrod, Matt Skinner, Jim Wilson, Michael Stevens.

The Swifts perform at the Holland Hotel.

Jim Wilson plays and sings at the Holland Hotel.

older songs such as "Navajo Rug." The patio outside the Century Grill also sponsors live music from groups such as the Swifts.

Marfa

When Donald Judd, modernist artist and sculptor from New York City, chose tiny Marfa, Texas, in 1979 as a place to live and work, he changed the town forever. Once a small, dusty town in the Big Bend, it is an artist's colony today and attracts art lovers from New York City, Dallas, and Houston who buy second homes there. Marfa is home to Judd's Chinati Foundation, and the Lannan Foundation awards a writer's residency there.

It was once best known as the location for the shooting of the movie *Giant* in 1956, when Elizabeth Taylor, Rock Hudson, and James Dean stayed at the Hotel Paisano during the filming. Marfa is also known for the mysterious Marfa Lights. These days, Marfa is described as hip and chic with an urban influence. Although Marfa has acquired a veneer of sophistication, much of the town still reflects a rural and ranching way of life. Many art galleries, festivals, and literary events draw crowds of tourists to Marfa.

The Lost Horse Saloon: Ty Mitchell

Ty Mitchell opened his Lost Horse Saloon in Marfa seven years ago. He first came to Marfa when he was sixteen, left to join the military, and returned when his tour of duty was over. Ty is well known in the Big Bend, and so is his dog Quatro. He lives in Marfa with his wife, writer Astrid Rosenfeld, who is widely published overseas.

The Lost Horse has been described as "rustic-chic," a term that would horrify Ty. Any Texan would feel right at home there; it is typical of any country bar in the state. The Lost Horse regularly features live music. Ty never has to call and book bands to come perform; they call him. He sees a change in the music

Ty Mitchell, proprietor of the Lost Horse Saloon, and his dog, Quatro.

scene in Marfa. "We had dance clubs, because we didn't have dance halls. They would go to the USO building and usually meet once a month. Like a rancher's ball or a Tejano ball. Each group had their own music and it was always country or it was Tejano. When Marfa started getting popular, young people came from out of town. And of course they brought their culture, and they introduced the town to a lot of music it wasn't used to hearing. Ended up, more bands coming out because of that," he said. When Ty has asked some of the bands what type of music they play, they cannot define it but describe it as a cross between two genres.

Ty has noticed that bands coming out of Nashville are winning country music awards and recording on country labels, but "there ain't enough country in them to fill up a thimble. As far as the vaqueros and cowboys, the music is pretty much the same. Like Irish folk music, it tells the story like the Tejano music. It's spawned from the same thing. You know: my dog died and the truck won't start, my girl died and the bank took all my stuff. That's what they sing about. You dance to it different, but that's always been here, and I don't see why it would have ever been anything different," Ty said.

When Ty was a teenager, the jukeboxes in town played Glenn Miller and big band music. Now his older customers will listen to 1950s rock and roll, but it is hard rock, punk, and heavy metal that bring in a packed house of young people.

It is difficult to gauge the popularity of a particular group in Marfa. "The problem is to figure anything out. We've got fifty-two weekends of an adult theme park. You know, I mean, it's just stupid. People standing in the middle of the street taking pictures and shit, acting like they ain't never seen a turkey before. You're driving and a cowboy goes through town with a trailer full of horses . . . geez, it's like he's got a parade, you know. We're like a ski resort that never closes but doesn't have a ski slope. Nobody gets the off season that lives here," he said.

In addition to groups that Ty thinks will have an appeal in Marfa, artists that come to the Chinati also sometimes appear as performance artists. Ty remembers a particularly memorable act he booked at the Lost Horse. "I had Conrad Friberg in here. His art is pretty cool. He does art with music. He has a pendulum with paper and paint under it. Then, he plays music to make the pendulum move. So each piece of art's different. He did a geometry tour, he called it. He brought a box and set it up on the stage. He got in there with a ukulele, a banjo, and a squeeze-box, and he sat in this box. The art people thought it was cool. They would take the chairs out on the dance floor to sit and watch him," Ty said.

Ty knew his regulars would not appreciate this performance. "I told him [Friberg], 'Look, if I just leave you, they'll tar and feather you at the least, and drag you out of town, so I'm gonna book a Tejano band, and they're going to play in between your music. Because I'm gonna have two different classes of people here, and I don't want them killing each other. But I've got to give these boys something besides that.' He said, 'Yeah, I get it. I understand it's kind of unique.'"

"I liked the guy. Hell, I had to kick one of the city councilmen out of the bar for six months because he wouldn't shut up. He kept going over there and hollerin' in the box," Ty explained. The ending to this story, according to the locals, is that the councilman not only shouted insults in the box but went up and poured his beer over the artist.

Obviously, running a bar in the Big Bend is not without drama. Ty remembers when he had to fight unruly customers. "You know, when I first opened this place I had to go to the ground three times a week for somebody. I was just whooping ass and takin' names. Then I didn't have a fight for almost two years. Them boys will hurt you," he said.

Marfa changes regularly because of publicity from national publications naming the town a vacation destination. "Marfa's a different town every six months, but damn sure every two years it's a completely

different town than it ever had been before. It's just a complete flip into something else in a different direction. People keep coming for a cheap vacation, beautiful country, and seeing the Big Bend. During spring break it is full of families," Ty said. The Lost Horse Saloon is a constant and authentic place in Marfa. It is difficult to imagine it would ever change.

Saint George Hall

Saint George Hall is adjacent to the Hotel Saint George and serves as the event space for the hotel. It is a large space that can regularly accommodate concerts and headliners for the various festivals.

In addition to Saint George Hall, the Capri has a large space attached to its restaurant. The historic USO Building, the Chinati Foundation, and the Hotel Paisano ballroom also host events.

Marathon

In Marathon, the Gage Hotel hosts musicians and bands, particularly in the summer at the height of the tourist season. Marathon is called "the gateway to the Big Bend," and many tourists stay there on the way to the park.

Eve's Garden, an organic bed-and-breakfast, is a unique place to stay in Marathon. The outdoor space and accommodations are centered around a beautiful garden of flowers and vegetables. It recently sponsored Turquoise Tuesdays with Neil Trammell of the Doodlin' Hogwallops, accompanied by other local musicians.

5

The Guitar Man and a Love Story

Michael Stevens

MICHAEL STEVENS DESIGNS and makes guitars owned by serious musicians such as Eric Clapton, Stevie Ray Vaughan, and Christopher Cross. From late 1986 to 1990, Michael was the senior design engineer of the Fender Custom Shop at Fender Musical Instruments Corporation, recruited by Fender with assistant John Pope to establish that department. He designed a double-neck guitar for Christopher Cross and the guit-steel for Junior Brown. "The Chris Cross guitar was designed by me about the time he won five Grammys. It got a nice little write up in *Billboard* magazine," Michael said. "The Clapton guitars were not designed by me, but were Fender Stratocasters built to Eric's specs off his old guitar Blackie with a couple of modern electronic additions. I made the necks and templates for production, assembled them both, and set them up to his specs."

In an interview in the *El Paso Times* from April 5, 2017, on the thirtieth anniversary of the Fender Custom Shop and the launch of eight limited edition guitars from eight of their original master designers known as Founders Design guitars, Michael told the story of the Clapton guitars. He was stymied by incorrect information that led to several failed attempts to

build the neck of the guitar. Finally, Clapton sent his guitar tech and his famous guitar Blackie. "I was so paranoid having that guitar, I would lock it in my office and keep it under my bed with a gun under my pillow. I didn't want that on my tombstone: 'The man who lost Blackie.'"

Later, these guitars were put up for auction for Clapton's Crossroads Foundation, established in 1997, which funded the residential drug and alcohol facility Crossroads Centre. In June 1999 lot number 62 sold for $107,000, the only nonvintage guitar to top $100,000, and in 1986, lot number 86 sold for $231,500, in the top three highest bids. These guitars had Michael's name on them and were listed in the Christie's auction catalogs as built by Michael.

Now he designs and builds custom guitars in a shop on his property outside Alpine, Texas. The formal name of the business is Stevens Electrical Instruments, and the website is StevensGuitars.com. In addition to being a master craftsman, he is also a well-respected musician.

When you meet Michael Stevens, it is hard to imagine that he has not always been in the Big Bend. In the customary cowboy hat, jeans, and well-worn

Michael Stevens, master guitar maker.

He worked on the Parker Ranch and others but spent most of his time on the Scharbauer Ranch. "He stayed with that almost to the war and then, like most cowboys, decided it wasn't enough money, then went to work for Western Union and World War II broke out," Michael said. Michael's grandmother said his father was caught three times trying to join the army and was sent home, being told that since he worked for Western Union, he was in the army already. "He spent the whole war in the Dakotas building telegraph lines for the air bases. There were all kinds of training bases up there and fighter squadrons and bombers."

Michael's father had also been to Marfa and Fort Davis when he worked for the Scharbauer Ranch, delivering donations to the Bloys Church Camp outside Fort Davis. "So, that's where the cowboy thing started and after the war he went back home and met my mom and they got married. Five kids later, he kept threatening to come back to Texas, but he never did. He never knew I got here; I hadn't gotten here by the time he died at age sixty-six."

The rural life with horses and his father's western dreams also influenced Michael's siblings. His brother Rick is a well-known farrier and now makes his own brand of horseshoes. He was also a ring steward at the All American Quarter Horse Congress for forty years, the largest single breed show in the world, and was scribe for the Pinto Horse Association and the National Reining Horse Association. He still lives a few miles outside Newcomerstown. Michael's three sisters also live in the area. The eldest and her daughter raise miniature goats and care for their youngest sister, who has Alzheimer's disease.

Just six months from high school graduation, Michael decided to go to Ohio State and major in general studies but ended up in art school. He was the assistant shop teacher in his senior year of high school and also taught mechanical drawing and American history. "Teachers all lived out in the country and because they'd get snowed in, or their car would break down or something would happen, I'd get called.

boots, the usual dress in the Big Bend, he just looks like a cowboy. But Michael was born in Coshocton, Ohio, in the nearest hospital to Newcomerstown, Ohio, in 1945. His mother was from Newcomerstown and his father from Cambridge, Ohio, also the home of Bill Boyd, better known as Hopalong Cassidy.

Michael's father wanted to be a cowboy, and horses were a part of his life. When his father was nineteen, Michael's grandparents gave him twenty dollars and a bus ticket to Midland so he could learn to be a cowboy.

"Banjos in the Cowcamp" session at the Cowboy Poetry Gathering.

I got about eighteen bucks a day, which in 1962 was okay," Michael explained.

Michael still dreamed of being a cowboy. "At some point, I was still into being a cowboy, but you couldn't wear those clothes to school. The kids looked at you like you're stupid because I was a football player and on the yearbook staff. But if you went with boots, and back then fringed jackets were hip for cowboys, they just looked at you like you were nuts."

After two years at Ohio State, Michael realized he was not happy in Columbus. He audited agriculture classes in addition to being on the Ohio State Army ROTC varsity rifle team for two years. When he left the university he was immediately drafted but classified as 1-Y, to be called only in time of war or national emergency, because of football injuries. "One knee is about to give out right now. From 1963, it's about dead. Hurts a lot. I'd gotten them both hurt in the last year of football. Played with the left hurt, taped up, and bandaged up. So, this one went first and then that summer I was chasing a cow and the other one went out. They put me back in the hospital. So, I had them both operated on within five or six months. Woody Hayes wouldn't let me play football at Ohio State because I wasn't big enough. I needed to be 220. Woody's from Newcomerstown, Ohio, and he could have been collaborating with my mother too. I don't know," Michael laughs.

He describes his decision to move west as wanderlust. His desire to come to Texas was fueled by his father's stories of his time in Midland. "I wanted to go to Texas from the time I was probably five and a half, I think," Michael said. However, he knew nothing about the Big Bend. That came about when he found the love of his life, Alice Griffin, at Texas Christian University in 1966. The couple followed a long and circuitous path for over twenty years before they finally had the chance of a happy ending.

Michael, his roommate John, and their vocalist Gayle were performing at the Fort Worth Botanic Garden when he first saw Alice. Gayle had been trying to set them up, but Michael refused to go on blind

dates. After a party that night, Michael and Alice began dating, only to break up. She married the man she was dating when Michael left Fort Worth to work in the oil fields in Midland. He was there for ten months until he realized he did not want to do that for the rest of his life. "A high school girl rammed into the back of my station wagon and they gave me three hundred dollars—and I fixed it with duct tape and a new plastic tail light cover. I bought a case of oil and came out to Berkeley to find out what was going on." Alice's family was also near Berkeley. "That year the family went to Anacortes, Washington, for Christmas. So, there I was stuck in Berkeley November of '67 and no Alice."

Michael heard she was divorced and kept in touch. He saw her every time he was in Fort Worth, even if only to say hello. "According to her girlfriend who did jewelry with her a lot of times, she talked about me a lot and she ruined a lot of relationships for me in Berkeley, but it didn't slow me down much, you know? As a bass player in a country band, I made do," Michael said.

Alice got married again, to an oilman, and was living in Fort Worth. She soon realized that he was very

controlling. He did not want her to see her friends and was very demanding. "Two months later she went up to his office in the petroleum building in Fort Worth and knocked on his door and he opened it up and he was there with his Italian silk tie and a Perry Ellis shirt pulled open at the collar. And she said, 'It's over!' and hit him in the face with a cream pie and left," Michael said.

Alice earned a master of fine arts degree from TCU and went on to teach jewelry making and metals there. Henry Hopkins at the Modern Art Museum of Fort Worth was her mentor and employer, and she also studied with renowned sculptor Harry Geffert. During this time, she met Donald Judd, whom she ended up working with in Marfa. By then, she was an accomplished photographer, jewelry maker, and potter.

Michael left Berkeley for Weatherford, Texas, where Alice was working as a bookkeeper and an assistant to the ranch owner. Michael was hired on as an assistant to train the Arabian horses, but by the time he arrived, Alice had left for Fort Worth. "She kind of stayed aloof for a while. I don't know when we saw each other. I don't know if she had cold feet. I have no idea. I stayed for four or five years working for Alan, and we traveled all over the country with Arabian horses. Then I moved from Weatherford. This was before the Weatherford boom," Michael said.

He moved to Austin for the vibrant music scene. "Stevie Ray Vaughan was just getting a name and the Thunderbirds were there. Eric Johnson, David Grissom, Omar and the Howlers, and everybody knew about me already from Berkeley. So, I get back there and pretty soon all those guys are my customers. When Stevie and Lonnie Mack did their double album, a blues album, I worked on Lonnie's guitar—the first and only time it was worked on," Michael said. "With two partners I finally bought a building in downtown Austin off of Twelfth Street right by the freeway." One of the partners suggested he should build something rather than just repair the instruments. "That's where I built the Christopher Cross guitar with the double neck that he got five Grammys with," Michael explained. He was also successfully performing with the Austin Lounge Lizards, who won the bluegrass contest at the 1983 Kerrville Folk Festival.

Then Alice moved to the Big Bend in the early 1980s to accept a job as an art counselor for the Davis Mountain Achievement Center, which became High Frontier, a residential treatment center and boarding school between Fort Davis and Alpine, serving adolescents between twelve and seventeen. She became the first resident counselor at the school. Michael visited her in Alpine in 1985 and proposed in 1986, the same year he got the job with Fender, and they moved to California and married at the end of 1987. They returned to Alpine in December 1990.

After living and working in the area for several years, they were able to buy their property. Michael then set out to build his shop. "When we set the steel up we had fifty people out here. We had a big electrical pole on this end with a buttress out from the top of it and then the steel went up. A couple of cowboys and Glenn, another buddy of mine, and a musician, Steve Bannock, put up five rows first. We'd poured the slab by then so we had rolling scaffolding and we could move back and forth. And then we had a big party, like an Amish barn raising, and Tommy Vaughan and Oscar, his Hispanic buddy, came out here and set up a chuck wagon right next to the slab. People started showing up on the designated day. We ate all three meals off the chuck wagon and then went in the house and played music all night," Michael remembers.

Paint booth.

The shop is an amazing space filled with templates for guitars and their parts, machinery to cut out the pieces, a professional paint booth, and two rooms in back where Michael does expert finishing on the instruments. Michael also had a shop in Alpine.

Alice continued making jewelry that was sold in galleries from Los Angeles to Santa Fe, pursuing her photography and becoming the owner of the One Way Plant Nursery in Alpine, specializing in native plants. After their twenty years of finding a way to permanently be together, their idyllic and creative lives were about to change forever.

In 2014, Alice was diagnosed with three brain aneurysms. Although two were successfully removed in Dallas, one was left. Her voice began to be affected. "They said the aneurysm is not what's causing her voice problems and it just kind of kept on going until

Michael and Alice. Courtesy of Michael Stevens.

the end, August 2016. But she was moving around and still walking and not talking much," Michael said. She was diagnosed with ALS, also known as Lou Gehrig's Disease, and was sent to Baylor for further tests. "She was just freaked out and just looked at me at breakfast and said clear as a bell: 'ALS is a death sentence.'" The year 2015 and most of 2016 were grueling for Michael and Alice. They began making trips to San Antonio to the ALS Association of Texas. "I got no work done out here almost. I got a little bit done, I can't remember when I got all the guitar bodies done and everything ready for everybody's guitars. When it comes time to build a guitar, there are three bases: there's the neck blank, the finger mold, and the bodies. I probably couldn't have gotten the

truss run cover on square, I had no concentration," Michael said.

While Alice was at High Frontier, she became nearly a mother to a girl named Amanda Chance. It was Amanda who came and took care of Alice. "Amanda saved my bacon. It would have been impossible to do it alone," Michael said.

Alice passed away at home on August 20, 2016. Her ashes are buried under two vitex trees close to the house. Michael continues to work on his guitars, performs with musicians in the area, and was active in the Cowboy Poetry Gathering in Alpine. This is where he will stay. "They're going to put me out there under the same trees. Dump my ashes out on a non-windy day and water me in along with our wedding rings she made."

6

The Radio Shows

THE RADIO STATIONS IN the Big Bend serve the areas of Alpine, Marfa, and Marathon. Alpine's KALP 92.7 FM defines itself as "live and local." In addition to music programming, the station also covers local sports and news. At one time, KALP played strictly country music but has since broadened its programming.

Jamming and Jawing with JR

JR Smith, host of the popular program *Jamming and Jawing with JR*, interviews musicians from the area and those who perform from elsewhere. "I get to interview some wonderful, talented folks here on my radio show of all levels from all over this area. Young and old, and we've got a bunch of wonderful live music venues in this area. Here's one of those musicians, right there. That's Sheriff Jim Wilson," JR said. Musicians come in to see JR to drop off their latest CD or to discuss their upcoming interview, as Jim Wilson has done.

JR is a seasoned broadcaster, announcing his first horse shows in the 1950s. "I produced and announced rodeos from California to Texas, to Missouri, Iowa, Kansas, and Nebraska. I was a color broadcaster on ESPN the four years they broadcast Mesquite Championship Rodeo. Still announce a horse show or a cutting or something from time to time, but have done sports radio color at various levels and have always been on the fringe of the music business somewhere, somehow," he said. His grandchildren attend a school where they can learn stringed instruments starting in the third grade, and JR has sent them instruments to learn on.

Although JR grew up in North Texas, he went to school in West Texas. "When my kids came along I had to go to town and get a real job. I'd worked on ranches," he said. JR worked in the fine paper business for thirty years and would travel every six weeks to El Paso. "Rather than them sending somebody to call on the printers, I was in specifications. I didn't call on printers, but instead of sending two different people, I would call on printers out there one day and call on the specification people the next day," JR explained. "When my youngest graduated from Texas Tech, I sent them out on the concrete and cubicles. I came back and took a job on a ranch north of Fort Davis and was up there a year. Got an opportunity down here and was director of the chamber of commerce

JR Smith, host of *Jamming and Jawing with JR*.

for six years." He is also an artist and painted one of the murals in town for the chamber of commerce.

JR has seen a blend of music here over the years that more accurately reflects the demographics of the Big Bend, which is 50 percent Hispanic. "For the Fourth of July, Fort Davis traditionally has Jody Nix and they play on the Saturday night closest to the Fourth of July. We're putting on a dance on Friday night with Max Baca and the Texmaniacs and Flaco Jiménez on Friday night for a dance up in Fort Davis. There will be a mix of the fans of both at both dances," he said. JR compared the events to the rodeo dances here in the 1970s and 1980s that featured two dance floors. "Over here is where the old timers dance and over there is where the young folks dance and they're commingling back and forth," JR said.

JR names musicians such as Johnny Rodriguez, Flaco Jiménez, and Los Lonely Boys who have successfully performed crossover music between genres, particularly in West Texas. "During Viva Big Bend, in the lobby at the Holland Hotel with Flaco Jiménez sitting on the couch there, they were flocking around him, getting his autograph," he said. JR is devoting an entire month to shows featuring the performers in Viva Big Bend, a mix of Anglo and Hispanic musicians. His radio show is popular because of the relaxed atmosphere. The interviews are conversations with musicians about their music.

Tejano Sundays

Robert Alvarez hosts the weekly program *Tejano Sundays*, which, like *Jamming and Jawing with JR*, is broadcast on KALP 92.7; Robert is on the air from 3:00 to 6:00 p.m. He was born and raised in Odessa, but his mother is from Marfa and his father is from Balmorhea. "I have ties to this area and I've been coming here since I was a kid. I've lived in Fort Davis for the last ten years," he said. "I do the long twenty-six-mile commute from over there to here, but it's quicker and much prettier than even the five-mile

commute I had when I was working in San Antonio because of the traffic. Here it's just pretty and you're just driving along."

Robert managed a radio station in San Antonio and then moved to Abilene as the director of the chamber of commerce before settling in the Big Bend. His radio show is very popular and the station is pleased with the response. The new owners brought back live disc jockeys instead of relying on automated or satellite radio, which "doesn't give you any regionality. So the new owners changed that. There are several shows that are on here now that are locally produced. Why this show was so successful is because we brought back Tejano music," Robert explained. "There are a million genres that cross over and a lot of people don't really understand the definition between them. Tejano is different than conjunto, which is different than norteño, which is different than regional Mexican. Conjunto music to me is the roots of Tejano music. It began way back with migrant workers who would have nothing but a broken-down accordion and a box guitar that was made out of something or other, cigar box guitar. But they would sing the classic songs, the traditional songs from Mexico that was typically mariachi music." Although these musicians did not have the typical instruments played in mariachi music, they still played the traditional favorites such as "Cielito Lindo." Then, in the 1950s and 1960s, there was the influence of *orquestra*, which added brass and became Tejano music with the addition of horns. Robert believes Sunny Ozuna was the musician who brought Tejano music to national attention. "So Sunny bridged that gap big-time, but that one song 'Talk to Me' really did it, gave more substance to the Mexican artist, to the Tejano artist, called the Chicano artist back then—another label," Robert said. "It got going and it got recognition. There are many icons like that. Little Joe is another one, and Ruben Ramos." To celebrate the first anniversary of the show and the first anniversary of the new ownership of the station, they booked Ruben Ramos to perform. The first year of the show was very successful.

Robert Alvarez,
host of *Tejano Sundays*.

"It's the program that generates the most income for the station, this little three-hour Tejano show that I do. We brought in this Grammy winner. He does the same thing as Sunny, he comes out in a white suit. He doesn't wear a hat but he always wears sunglasses," Robert said.

Even with the rise in popularity of Tejano music in the Big Bend, norteño is still very popular. Robert explains the enduring popularity of Tejano music: "There's joy in doing this type of music. Some folk music delivers a true, strong message and there are messages in the lyrics in Tejano music, but mostly it's just joy. It's fun music, a kind of party music. Even if it may be talking about, 'Oh, I lost my love . . . boo hoo, boo hoo,' the rhythm and the backing behind it is danceable. To me, it's trying to lift your spirit. It may be talking about something that's tragic or whatever but the groove that's in there, you can't help but to just bob your head or dance."

When Tejano music added horns and a brass section, it deviated from norteño style, which always had an accordion and a bajo sexto. Robert explained the bajo sexto as being just a differently tuned guitar. In addition, there will be a bass, drums, and sometimes a lone saxophone. The addition of horns set Tejano apart from conjunto and norteño music. Robert credits the iconic musicians of the 1960s Chicano movement, such as Sunny Ozuna and Little Joe, among others, for adding the horns that changed the sound of norteño. "It wasn't just accordion. It was brighter. To me, it was livelier, but not in the sense that it wasn't lively before, it was just that with the horns, compared to the accordion, that the timbral sounds, which you hear through your ear, are just brighter. And when they did that it was amazing," Robert said. There was another change in the 1980s for Tejano music when synthesizers were incorporated. Robert credits Joe Lopez, Jimmy Gonzalez, and Grupo Mazz for adding these synthesizers, although they had been used somewhat in the 1960s. "It was mostly the Moog organs and Hammond and B-3 that they used in sixties rock, and there were some Tejano acts that would

do that but it was like copying the guitar [singing] and then you hit with the B-3, like that. In the seventies it was used a little bit more, but synthesizers grew as well and they got the brass sounds on it. So if you couldn't afford to hire, or didn't want to pay for a full brass section, you now had synthesizers that took its place," Robert said. "A synthesizer also can provide electric pianos and strings, which can give more depth without having a big stage and a large orchestra. Mazz were among the first to use the synthesized strings. That's Tejano music."

Another emerging form of music is banda, which is most popular in Mexico. Robert describes the sound as almost like carnival music. What sets it apart is the tuba, which does the bass line and the horns. It is an older form of music and does not use anything electronic except amplifiers. All true banda groups feature the tuba. The style of music is lively and bright and it is popular as dance music. "This is like hopping around. The couple will dance very close together and it's literally hopping the whole time. But they'll work up a steam and I've seen young people do it. I've seen old people do it. They really enjoy it and maybe that's the attraction of banda music, that they like the hopping and dancing and you're really excited. Almost like, oddly enough, techno in English where you're just jumping around. Same thing, but you've got your partner," Robert said.

The continued success of *Tejano Sundays* ensures that Tejano music remains entrenched in the Big Bend.

Marfa Public Radio KRTS, 93.5 FM, broadcasting from Marfa, also broadcasts on KDKY 91.5 in Marathon, KRTP 91.7 in Alpine, and KXWT 91.3 in Midland-Odessa. The station offers an extensive and innovative schedule of local music programming from classical to jazz, bluegrass, Tejano, and norteño.

Dos Horas con Primo

Remijio "Primo" Carrasco and William Quintana cohosted the radio show *Dos Horas con Primo* on

Primo Carrasco of *Dos Horas con Primo.*

KRTS, the only Spanish-language music show in the region. It is now cohosted by Primo and Tim Johnson. Primo acquired his nickname when he worked on the railroad. "Everywhere they call me Primo now. I started getting 'Hey, Primo! Hey, Primo, come,' so everybody called me that. Now I'm Primo everywhere," he said.

Primo has lived in Marfa since 1972 and is from Ojinaga, Mexico. He believes the differences in music types are based not only on the instruments played, but also on the sound and the songs. Since he is from Ojinaga, he is very familiar with the Ojinaga Sound. "Norteño is from accordion. They used to call it

toloche instead of a bass and since it was norteño, there was the accordion. We've got bajo sexto, guitar, and toloche. In some norteño, they use just the toloche, bajo sexto, and guitar. In Ojinaga norteño they use bass, saxophone, accordion, guitar, and sometimes drums," Primo said. He also noted the difference between norteño and mariachi, which typically has eight or nine players.

Primo plays the guitar and sings, frequently with musician David Beebe of Marfa. David is the former owner of the popular bar and grill Padre's, which also featured live music. "It's weird because when we started he didn't know Spanish and I didn't know

William Quintana, cohost of *Dos Horas con Primo*.

English and he didn't believe me! When I retired from the railroad here in Marfa, they offered me some jobs. But I have to apply, right? I have to fill out the forms, the applications. When they asked how many years of school, in English, no? Spanish? None? I didn't have any school, not even in English or Spanish. You know, a little bit, I can read a lot of English, but the minute when I read a paper, I don't know the meaning of the words," he explained. When Primo began playing the guitar, he only knew one chord and the musicians he played with only knew one song. Then he came to the United States, went to Fort Worth, and was hired on at the railroad.

"There was a mariachi guy in the railroad and he wanted me to sing. I was so shy that I didn't want to, but it was me and him. He said, 'You play guitar?' I said, 'Poquito.' I started playing guitar and then later on my wife joined a choir in church so she invited me and I said, 'No, I don't want to be there.' Fine, but you know how the ladies are," Primo laughed. "So we had to do the choir and then from there it happened that this couple got married and they wanted a song about marriage. It's a song in Spanish, 'Anillo de Compromiso,' the compromise ring. So the sisters, the nuns, asked me if I could sing and I said yes. So, I'm singing by myself, so from there on everybody that has an anniversary, a marriage, they want me to sing that song, 'Anillo de Compromiso.'"

At an event for a local resident, Primo performed with a large group as a solo artist and sang. That led David Beebe and his business partner to ask Primo to perform at Padre's since they wanted Spanish music. "They called me and said, 'Hey, Primo, want to sing at Padre's?' I said, yeah, I should like to go sing there, but I thought it was in a group. When I got there they said, 'Okay, Primo.' It was by myself. So, I started singing and imagine two hours singing. I don't know how to entertain people. So, singing, singing, singing," he said. Then he began playing events with David.

Primo's cohost William Quintana grew up in Marfa during the 1940s and 1950s, attending the Blackwell School, called "the Mexican school" when Hispanic and Anglo students were segregated. When he attended high school, it was a mostly Anglo student body. In retirement he has become a knowledgeable historian and is a valuable resource for local history.

Will brings a photograph of his grandfather's Saint Cecilia's Jazz Band Orchestra, who performed at the USO Building during the 1930s and World War II. "As far as I know, my grandfather named it Saint Cecilia's Jazz Band Orchestra. My grandfather was a Methodist. It's kind of strange that he would name it after a Catholic saint. There was no Tejano music back then. No Tex-Mex. Nothing like that. So, they played jazz. My dad loved the big band sounds of the forties. Tommy Dorsey, Glenn Miller. That's what they loved, so that's what they played," he said.

Primo and Will discuss the types of music that are part of mariachi music, corridos, ballads based on poetry and narrative that reflect history and socially current topics, and *huapango*, which is typically folk music and dance in the *son huasteco* sound. Primo has tried to show some musicians how to play huapango, and although they are very talented on the bass and guitar, they are unable to produce that distinct sound. Meanwhile, *Dos Horas con Primo* ensures the preservation of valuable musical oral history.

7

A Life in Music

Juan Tarango Martinez

THE FIRST TIME WE met Juan Martinez was in the large outbuilding in back of his home in Marfa. His shop in the front was where he was refinishing cabinets for a remodeling job. This building is also home to his recording studio and control booth, a room where his accordions and guitars are stored that also has comfortable chairs and a sofa. He is most proud of his recording studio and has all the equipment he needs to produce CDs of his own band and others who come to record.

He knew when he was six that he wanted to play music. "I saw a small conjunto, a block away, and the sound of that music just fascinated me. There was this guy playing the accordion and I heard the accordion over all the instruments, that and the bass guitar, and I immediately was drawn to it. I convinced my mother to go and take me, my grandfather was here too, and he just loved music. So, we walked over," Juan said. Each of the musicians had a separate amplifier, so the sound carried down the block. Juan's grandfather had asthma and was having difficulty breathing, but he asked the band to play the song "Indita Mia" so he could dance with Juan's grandmother, who was a Native American from the Mescalero Apache tribe. "That was

my inspiration when I saw them dancing. They were in their late seventies and they were dancing even though he was having an asthma attack," Juan said. "He wanted to finish that song. They were both tired. It just made me realize that music makes people happy, and man, they were ecstatic to hear that song, and I guess he hadn't heard it in years, especially from a live band. I wanted to make people feel the same way," he said.

When he visited a cousin in Morton, a small town in Texas near Lubbock, Juan was able to watch him play the guitar and asked whether he would teach him. Within a week, he was already strumming chords. "I remember coming back and I started banging on coffee cans, whatever the heck I could find. There was an old shoe rack and I remember sticking the coffee cans on it and making a bunch of noise; they were looking at me like, oh boy. My grandfather told my mother that I had talent, that I was going to become a musician. She just kind of blew it off," Juan said. He was ten when he got his first Beatles drum set, which had one large bass drum, a tom-tom, and a snare. "I got some pallets that my dad had there and I stacked them and I made a little stage. I wanted my brother to be a musician so bad. They wanted to play on the bicycle and they didn't want to, I guess they never had my vision until later, but I kind of forced them into that. That's why they're all into music now," Juan said.

The same band he saw when he was six continued to play at parties but later broke up. Juan was their first drummer when they reunited. That was his first gig, playing the drums, but Juan found that boring. He was still attracted to the accordion. The accordionist loaned the instrument to Juan and taught him finger placement. "I started playing, very primitive. I just loved it. I borrowed that accordion from him maybe for two years or so, until I sort of got the hang of it," he said. Juan is completely self-taught on all the instruments he plays; although he cannot read music, he plays by ear.

His mother bought him a big blue accordion that reminded him of the geek character on the television show *Family Matters*. "It reminds me of Urkel, you know? I guess that's when I became a nerd because nerds play accordions. That thing was heavy! I couldn't even carry the damn thing. It was huge, hanging off this skinny kid," Juan said. That accordion was sky blue and Juan says it looked like a bowling ball. He proudly shows us his accordions: large, glitzy, beautiful instruments made by Gabbanelli. "This is the Cadillac of accordions. I sold a house here in town and the first opportunity I got, I paid five thousand dollars apiece for these. Brand new. Nobody has even played them or touched them. They came direct from the factory. Oh, man! I think I sucked all the new smell out of them just when I opened them. That was like dying and going to the big stage up in the sky, you know? Those were my first professional accordions," he said.

He was performing with different bands at the age of eleven, playing gigs that lasted sometimes until 3:00 or 4:00 in the morning. The musicians took him under their wing and taught him how to play bass and guitar. "That's where they started molding me and I learned a lot of the old-school conjunto songs. Not really too much Tex-Mex. It was just the old conjunto," Juan said. Even though he learned to play other instruments, he always returned to the accordion.

From an early age, Juan and his brother worked. Juan has an extraordinary work ethic. "My parents used to find yard work for me. Of course, I never kept any of the money. They would take me and I would clean chicken coops for three bucks. Not fun, you had feathers on you and dust. It was just horrible. I used to do that and I used to work at different ranches feeding cattle. I would help them round up. My brother worked at a ranch, the older one. He used to take me along. We were just pushed into it, doing ranch work and fixing fences and so forth," he said. "We really didn't have much of a childhood because it was always work. Then when the music came along I started noticing you could get fifty bucks in three or four hours." Juan also worked during Christmas break on his uncle's ranch gathering pecans and climbing trees to shake them down. "We had no Christmas break, we were gone working. After that, we would be chopping weeds in the cotton fields. I would be doing the ranch jobs, and chicken coop cleaning, and you name it. Everything I could do to earn money," Juan said. When he was in junior high and high school, he sold hogs and rabbits through 4-H and FFA, and that money went to buying instruments. Juan still considers himself an odd-jobber, but he supported his family solely through his music for thirteen years. "I had to get a job at a grocery store for a while there, and then with the National Park Service, twelve years, then here at the Chinati Foundation," he said. He is now the certified welding teacher at Marfa High School.

Juan's daughter has started singing with his band. Juan has had two bands; the first was Grupo Exito de Marfa, and now his band is Grupo Alturas. His daughter plans to go to college but wants to return to the area. Juan is encouraging her to learn how to be a sound or recording engineer, because that will provide the opportunity to make the most money. He learned to produce CDs from his sound engineer in Odessa, who gave him a list of the basic equipment he would need, but some of that equipment cost $20,000 to $30,000. "How am I going to do that? I got on eBay

Left to right: Cornelio Vega, Juan Martinez, Anastacio Milan.

and some of this stuff is brand new but used. Even that machine is outdated and it's still over eight thousand dollars," Juan said. Over time, he has painstakingly assembled all the equipment and has groups coming from as far away as Midland-Odessa to record in the much smaller town of Marfa because of the laid-back atmosphere.

Grupo Alturas is very versatile in addressing the musical tastes of the area. For people who like acoustic music, they do not take the drums but will perform with the accordion, the bajo sexto, and the upright bass, which is traditional Mexican music. "That is a traditional norteño that we'll play and the traditional conjunto, but it's way different. If you throw in a saxophone, it changes the dynamics. We alternate accordion, and we also like to play country. We are mixing what has already been mixed and tinkered with; now we were playing an old-style norteño, Tejano, conjunto, mixed with country," Juan said.

The second time we see Juan in his studio, he has invited Anastacio Tacho Milan, from Alpine, who is retired and writes a column for the *Zavala County Sentinel* in Crystal City; and Cornelio Vega, who works as a DJ at dances and events and was a long-haul coast-to-coast truck driver. Juan and Cornelio believe Anastacio has an encyclopedia of music in his head.

Anastacio begins by pointing out that Spanish music is a blend of everything, and it started in Mexico. "You cannot neglect those composers, those singers and musicians from the past; they are legends. For example, José Alfredo Jiménez is the author of ranchera, La Musica Ranchera. Ranchera is that fast-moving music many Hispanic Mexicanos dance to, like the polka," he said. He went on to explain boleros as more romantic, slow dance music. He names the romantic elements of boleros: lovers and couples. "A bolero is a type of rhythm that calls for romance, when you're courting somebody, it has a lot of passion involved. When somebody's heartbroken or when you want to win a woman over, *conquistarla* (to conquer

her), you will sing her a bolero. You win her heart with those nice, sweet tunes," Juan said.

Corridos tell a story, and the instrumental sounds are reminiscent of polkas. "The Germans brought the polka to America. That's a more fun type of fast-paced music. The accordion, the guitar, and so forth. No voices now. It's just the polka. Mexican music has everything in one bag," Anastacio said. "That's the marvelous thing about Tejano music. You identify that but it comes from all these types of different music that originated in Mexico. Things that go back even before the revolution. It's not only Mexican music and that's it."

As a DJ, Cornelio finds he is playing a lot of banda music, which is popular with the younger people, but there is always a demand for norteño in the area. Techno music is comparable to banda. "With banda music, that's one of my biggest turnoffs, I'm not putting it down but it's narcocorridos. It's about how much beer you can drink, how many people you can kill," said Juan. "Banda is all over. In fact, in San Antonio they've got stations that play nothing but banda, you've got stations that play nothing but norteño, you've got stations that play nothing but Tejano, and anything that you can think of," said Anastacio. "That's what's happening in the Odessa, the El Paso area. That's all you hear on the radio nowadays. It's very rare that you hear in four hours of music a song from Conjunto Primavera or one of these norteños like Los Tigres because they're playing all of that banda stuff," added Cornelio.

Cornelio and Juan discuss the very different characteristics of Tejano and norteño music: "Tejano is completely brass and synthesizers. That's what makes the difference in Tejano music. The Tejano industry is all brass, electric guitar, synthesizers, and of course, every other instrument. Norteño is saxophone and bajo sexto," said Cornelio. "Norteño has one brass, and the reeded instruments, which are the basic ones and the accordion. You have to have the accordion in norteño music. Then they add the saxophone and the bajo sexto, which is your twelve string bass guitar

Juan Tarango Martinez.

combo. Instead of the upright bass, they now use the electric four string bass. So that's your norteño," said Juan.

Since much of the Big Bend was originally part of Mexico, there was the matter of the popularity of Mexican music on this side of the new border in the early days. "Well, in my time it's always been accepted. I'm forty-four years old so in my time everything has come through," said Cornelio. In the 1950s and earlier, Marfa, Alpine, Marathon, Fort Davis, and Presidio were very small towns. There was access to only the radio. Juaréz, Ojinaga, and XERF in Ciudad Acuña, Mexico, had radio stations with such strong frequencies, they could be heard states away.

XERF, the home of Wolfman Jack, could be heard across the United States.

"We heard music since our roosters started crowing outside. Grandma would turn on the music, listen to the announcers from that radio station. It was a very prominent radio station that everybody would hear. They would play, of course, Mexican music, and they would have different portions throughout the day, different programs. We had access to Mexican music for one hour through KVLF radio station in Alpine. That was the only station. There was no Tejano music during that time," Anastacio said.

Conjunto is the oldest music from Mexico, and its roots are apparent in the other genres. "Conjunto

is like your Flaco Jiménez type of music. Now, that type of music involves four people, which is bajo sexto, a bass guitar, a drum set, and an accordion, and that's it. And it's very traditional. It was music that originated in the border towns," said Cornelio. In the Rio Grande Valley, in McAllen, San Antonio, and Del Rio along that portion of the border in Texas, conjunto is still very popular. In the Big Bend, it is not as popular. "It's known as *musica en la cantina*, bar music, because that's where they would play that music. Here is not really big on conjunto, never has been. Now, you go from Abilene, Lubbock, Dallas, Houston, all that area, to San Antonio, and even in the Valley, you do have Tejano music. You have the old-school Tejano and then you have the newer type of Tejano, like Jay Perez and Chente Barrera, Little Joe," he said.

They credit Sunny Ozuna and Baldemar Huerta, perhaps better known as Freddy Fender, for breaking the barrier into the Anglo community when they began singing bilingual Tejano and oldies music. "They are two prime examples of what used to prevail at the time. Everybody's got their stories. Sunny Ozuna is a very versatile, talented musician. You name it, he sings it. Mariachi, Tejano, the most beautiful song that I have ever heard, 'Talk to Me,'" said Anastacio. "You have to get your foot in the door, then you can do what you want," said Juan.

In the recording studio.

Anastacio is a gold mine of music history and offers insightful observations about the evolution of music in the area. "Some of my stories indicate being in the right place at the right time, having a lot of blessing, good luck, and having that inspiration to continue forward. You cannot achieve or fulfill anything sitting down and waiting for people to come to you. I have learned that from experience. You've got to go out there, go reach for the doors, open the doors, and if that doesn't work, there's a saying in Spanish, 'Una puerta se cierra, otra abrc,'" he said. "A door closes, another opens."

Juan's band members in Grupo Alturas are his family: his brother, nephew, nieces, and daughters.

He laughs when he compares them to the Partridge family. "When we show up it's like a family reunion. All of my family traveled together and that includes my parents. They're elderly and we have to take them. They still love to listen to the Tejano music and the norteño music that we play. They still get out there and dance. They enjoy that," Juan said. They have worked hard at becoming adept in many genres of music. They are asked to play a very wide variety of music at their gigs. "The Cupid Shuffle, the Electric Slide, but then I've got all these elderly people that want me to play Flaco Jiménez. They want me to play norteño. And I've got all these other Tejano people who want me to play Joe Lopez, Grupo Mazz. It never fails, George

Juan Tarango Martinez.

Strait must be played at every dance," Juan said. It is a continual process of learning new music, new songs, rehearsing, and performing. "It's hard for us musicians, because I cannot, up to this day, go to a dance and enjoy it and just dance. It's all about listening to what they're playing, how they play it, what I can learn from them, what mistakes I can catch. And you know, I can't enjoy myself. I am very critical, and it's hard for me to enjoy music," said Cornelio.

Anastacio comments on the timeless quality of music: "The remarkable thing, and the same applies to English music, is that Spanish Mexican-style music never dies. You can hear a song from way back in 1920 and you will still enjoy it, and it might portray something about some relationship going on with lovers or whatever. Different elements of life that exist even today. You're familiar with all of that," he said. Anastacio is writing a book about music and musicians. "We have to do something that will be recognized as something outstanding on our behalf. We don't represent us individually, we represent our people, a lot of people," he said. "I'm pretty sure that I promote and I'm an advocate of recognizing these good people that have contributed, and it's a culture that's lost. We're Americans, but we have our own history, our own background that you identify as *cultura*."

Juan is a happy man because he has been able to do what he loves most—music—while raising a family. He still has the emotional response and awe for music that he had at the age of seven. "I don't think there's any damn drug that'll give you that high. It makes you feel as if you're on top of the world for those few minutes. When I'm singing, I think about my childhood when I really wanted to become somebody, and then, I can't believe it. I have to pinch myself and say, 'Look where the hell you are, Juan. Look what you're doing!'" he said. "Makes me feel as if I have accomplished something bigger than what I thought because now, I am the mentor for not only my brother but my kids and my nephews. I sucked them into this big whirlpool and now they're part of it. I never imagined that I would have kids and see them playing. I look at them and I get emotional. My tears come out."

8

The Cowboy Poetry Gathering, Alpine

THIS EVENT DRAWS HUNDREDS of people every year to hear the poetry, music, and stories of the West. In addition to Alpine, there are annual Texas gatherings in Fredericksburg—called the Hill Country Cowboy Gathering—the Central Texas Gathering in Early, and the South Texas Gathering in Seguin. The National Cowboy Poetry Gathering in Elko, Nevada, draws thousands of people every year. The mission of these gatherings is to preserve the traditions, stories, and music of the cowboys and ranchers who are an integral part of the rural West. Folklorists, historians, poets, and musicians gather with the general public to share their music and poetry. In the program for this year's Gathering at Alpine, the committee stated: "The Texas gathering was the second such event to begin, Elko, Nevada being the first. As these two events led the way and other gatherings began around the west, a tribe began to form. Performers came from large and small ranches to find that there were others who shared their love and respect for a way of life."

Don Cadden, the president of the Gathering, explains the history: "In 1985, some folklorists decided that the old cowboy poems were being lost. They weren't written down a lot so they were being forgotten. So they contacted other folklorists across the country and said, 'Find people in your area, working cowboys and ranchers, people that know these old poems. Let's bring them to Elko, Nevada.'" In January 1985 in Elko, Nevada, during extremely cold weather, four or five thousand people came to attend the Gathering. The connection to Alpine was a ranch wife named Barney Nelson. "She was one of the people to go up there. Barney went to it and after the second year said we need to do this in Alpine. They started the one here in 1987. It was the second oldest Gathering in the country. She had some of the people she had met around the country come in, and it was very, very small, to just share stories with each other. From that it grew into what it is now," Cadden said.

The thirty-third annual Gathering in Alpine, Texas, drew over sixty poets and musicians from Texas and California as well as other states and Canada. Cadden and his committee sent out a letter informing the performers and sponsors of their decision to make this Gathering the last. As is the case with many organizations with long histories, the membership is aging out, and attempts to recruit younger members to the committee have been unsuccessful, although they have attracted younger attendees. "It's definitely an older audience, an older performing group. Our goal is to keep it very authentic. A lot of the Gatherings have become festivals," Cadden said. The hotels no longer gave any discounts for the meeting, although every hotel room and RV park in Alpine was completely booked for the event.

Difficulties arose with the venue at Sul Ross State University. Although the administration was supportive, the faculty and staff, on the whole, were not. When the Alpine Chamber of Commerce cut funding for the Gathering, the decision, although painful, was made to bring it to an end.

Since then, however, interest has arisen in preserving the tradition, and there are efforts underway to bring it back next year. At this writing, the future of the Alpine Cowboy Poetry Gathering looks hopeful.

Every Gathering features a full program of musical and educational sessions, offered to standing-room-only crowds. In 2018 there were ninety-two sessions over two days in classrooms at Sul Ross.

"Most of the performers are not professionals," Cadden explained. "They're ranchers, working cowboys. They are in some way tied to agriculture, to ranching. They may have had to move to town for a different job but still in their hearts they have a background in the western way of life. That's who we try to bring together and the whole committee votes on who we invite, but we will invite a working cowboy that's a pretty good poet before we will invite somebody who doesn't know which end of a cow eats, even if they're a great poet or a great musician."

A clear distinction is made between country music and western music. Western music is the music brought by cowboys to the ranches and ranges of the West. Gene Autry, Roy Rogers, and the Sons of the Pioneers are more current examples of those who preserve the songs sung around campfires, at ranches, and on the range. They are cowboy songs. They are also an oral history of the settlement of the West. When asked what distinguishes western from country music,

the musicians interviewed all said they were very different, that western music is romantic, even current western songs.

Don explained that historical western music started in the mid-1860s after the Civil War and continued until the trail drives of the late 1880s. "People would be out on the trail for months at a time and something would happen and a story would be told about it and put to rhyme because it's much easier to remember a story when it rhymes," he said. "When I first got into it you would go to a Gathering and you would hear eighty percent of the old, traditional

Don Cadden and Pam Cook.

poems and songs. Now, you probably hear ten percent of that. So much has been written in the last thirty or forty years. It is current, but in the traditional manner." Don names some of the old historic songs: "The Zebra Dun," "Strawberry Roan," "Tying Knots in the Devil's Tail," "Little Joe the Wrangler," and "Spanish is a Loving Tongue." These songs and the old poetry serve as the oral history of the West. Authenticity in the current poems and songs is most important. "You can tell immediately in the newer poetry that's been written, if somebody is talking about something that they know about from the ground up rather than something that they read books about and trying to write a poem about it. The truth comes out immediately,"

Don and his wife, Pam Cook, have lived in the Big Bend for eleven years. In 1966 when Don was twenty, his summer job as a brakeman with Southern Pacific Railroad, going from Sanderson to Valentine with overnight layovers, caused him to fall in love with the Big Bend. "I was twenty years old, in college facing the draft. There was just no way I could move out here."

Over the years, I came back and came back every chance I got." It was through the Gathering that he met and made friends with the participants. "I would come out and do day work on ranches out here, the big ranches," he said.

He and his good friend Apache Adams leased ranches together, and when Don was able to retire, he and Pam moved to Alpine. "Luckily, I had a wife who was willing to move out here, because a lot of women aren't. We have been very happy here," Don said. Pam did have to adjust to another way of life after living in the Austin area for thirty years. She missed the close friendships and her church community. "We'd been here less than a year and my daughter had our first grandchild in Houston, which is nine and a half hours away," Pam said. "That would have been the deal breaker probably if she'd had it before we left the Austin area, but I make a lot of trips to Houston. It's such a long trip that I would spend a day or two in Austin visiting friends, going to H-E-B or Costco. I could do that, get that taste of it, then come back here and not miss it in any way."

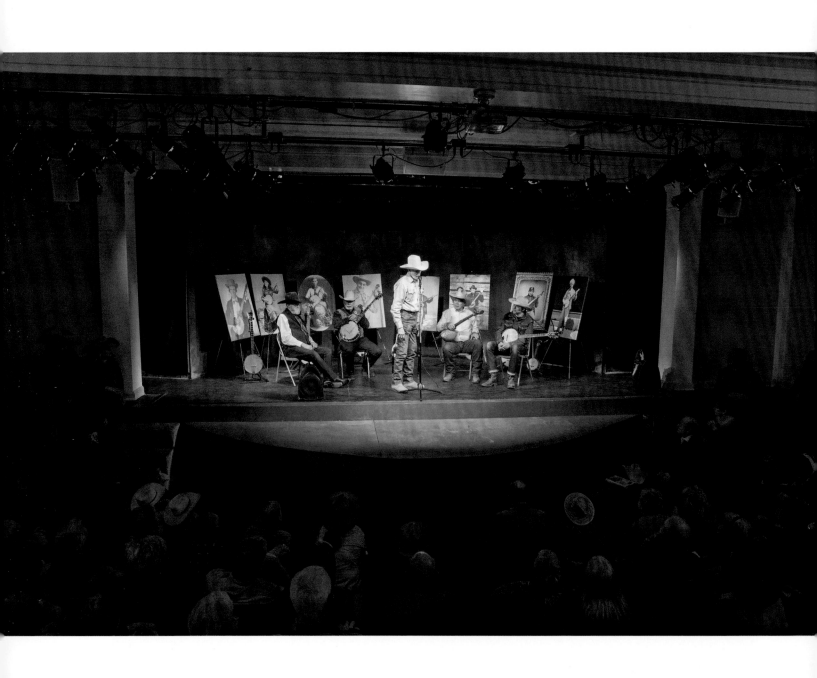

Pam was asked to join the committee for the Gathering and she concentrated on fund-raising. "When we came on, we were paying maybe a hundred-dollar stipend, and a little bit for a daily per diem, and gas money for the performers and that didn't nearly cover it. I worked for nonprofits my entire career and had done a lot of fund-raising events and just fund-raising in general. Don had done that too. So when we asked them, 'Why don't you do this?' they said, 'Oh, we don't ask for money. We don't want to ask for money. That's not the ranch way,'" she said.

Don and Pam realized there was a lot of potential in acquiring donors, particularly businesses that would like to have their names attached to the Gathering as sponsors. Since the Gathering was already a 501(c)(3), an official nonprofit, the money raised was tax deductible. Pam also coordinated the volunteers, and then she was voted in as a member of the committee. "Sponsorships have made the Gathering so much more solvent. We're able to pass along that money directly to the performers. So everything that comes in—we don't have any staff or anything like that—everything that comes in helps to support the Gathering," Pam said.

For two days, starting at 7:30 a.m., a chuck wagon breakfast at Kokernot Field in Alpine feeds over two hundred people. Next, sessions begin at Sul Ross State University, sporting titles such as "Stay Out of the Wire," "Up the Trail," "Cowboy Heroes," and "So You

Saturday night performance at the Gathering.

Banjo session at the Gathering, Sul Ross State University, Alpine, Texas.

Want to Marry a Cowboy." These well-attended sessions run all day. Don was a presenter at the sessions "Old Friends," "Long Days and Short Nights," "Tied Hard and Fast," "A Cowgirl and Her Heroes," "Shank of the Evenin'," and "God Bless Texas."

We attended "Banjos in the Cowcamp," introduced by Michael Stevens, where five accomplished musicians—Dale Burson, Allan Chapman, Pipp Gillette, Andy Hedges, and Michael Stevens—presented a program on the history of the different types of banjos and performed some songs. The overflow crowd was sitting on the floor and the stairs and standing three deep along the back of the room.

Washtub Jerry

Washtub Jerry is the performance name of the sole washtub bass musician in the Big Bend. When asked for his last name, he says it is Jerry and his first name is Washtub. He also performed at the Gathering. Jerry

earned two engineering degrees from New Mexico State University and has been an employee of the University of Texas at the McDonald Observatory outside Fort Davis for forty-eight years. He is the chief engineer at the McDonald Laser Ranging Station. He and Jane, his wife of fifty-three years, have raised a family in the Big Bend.

He was raised in Alamogordo, New Mexico, but identifies himself as a "full-blown Texan." His father was an engineer and his mother was a music teacher. His interest in music began in church. "What really started me liking music is being a snot-nosed kid in the Methodist Youth Sunday evening choir, where we would kick the preacher out of the pulpit and we would sing songs out of the Cokesbury hymnal. I just wanted to be somebody with the group," he said. He loved two-, three-, and four-part harmonies. Barbershop quartet and bluegrass music attracted him because of the harmonies.

He played first-chair bassoon in the band and orchestra at Alamogordo High School. Some people assume he went from the upright bass to the washtub bass, but he was never attracted to playing the upright bass. Jerry's mother was the only accordion teacher in Alamogordo and started youth and adult accordion bands. He felt he was a mediocre accordionist and didn't enjoy it. He could not sight-read music, although he was the first chair in the band. He would listen to the second chair, his best friend, and look at the music, and then found he could play it the second time. "That's the way I got through: by the skin of my teeth. I did not have any appreciation because I was struggling, and nobody ever said to me, 'Jerry, there are some people in the world who are best suited to be a support person,'" he said.

His mother suggested the washtub bass, since an old family friend had built one and played it. She described it as a string and a pole and said he could do the same. Jerry was seventeen and ignored the suggestion for five years. He was playing the ukulele then with two other ukulele players. He jokes that while he was the one in college, his mother was the one who was getting smarter. "I switched, not realizing that the first twelve years of playing that washtub bass, nobody would let me join them. There was a good reason, because I sucked and I understood that. Anybody that plays any musical instrument understands the concept, if you suck, nobody's going to ask you to join them. Duh. If you practice you get better. Well, so I practiced. It took me a dozen years," he said. His friends had a band and Jerry wanted to be part of it. He would turn on the radio and try to get the washtub and the radio music to work together. "I didn't hate my fellow musicians. I hated the concept that I wasn't there. So, I said, 'I'll show you. I'm going to practice and I'm going to get good. I'm going to get so good, you're going to ask me to play with you.' And they did," he said.

He describes the washtub bass as a "heritage instrument," tracing its origins to the west coast of Africa. "We call that an African earth bowl. There's a hole in the ground, animal hide over that, taut, and then a rawhide string up to a tree limb. They didn't treat it as a musical instrument or a drum. This is the part where I had to have help. I found those things and then I started asking historians, well, what did they do with it? Here's the consensus: it is believed that the tribe person would tap on that a particular rhythm. Something that was meaningful. They had rhythms," he said. The deep vibrations emanating from the ground were also a form of communication, Washtub believes.

The washtub bass became popular in the music of Appalachia and in early cowboy music. It is also used in the zydeco music of South Louisiana. He was invited to perform at the New Orleans Jazz Fest for two years. He has found that he is a welcome addition to performing bands. "I was taken into several places by an accordion-playing friend of mine and he knew the band. The bass players lit up because they understood and they said, 'Come play!'" he said. "Here's why: they understood that I play the elephant part [singing

Washtub Jerry.

bass sound effect]. And these cats have been trapped and gritting their teeth trying to play the foundation when really, what do they want to do? They wanted to go up the neck [singing], playing these really fun bass runs. Well, the bands are going to say to them to play the foundation. So, they pass the foundation to me and they have the time of their life that they're not usually permitted to do."

Jerry has played with a norteño band for nearly three years as the only Anglo. He became skilled in Mexican music. When he was at a music camp at the Silver Dollar City branch in Missouri, he met three marimba players and asked to play with them. They refused for three days because he had not looked over their songs and could not read music, but they finally relented. "They asked me to perform with them all the rest of their presentations because I could. And they were baffled, but they accepted the fact that even though I don't read music I knew those songs," he said.

He has also performed as the feature musician in the Midland-Odessa Symphony Orchestra. "We did an audition and I know it was an audition. What I didn't realize is almost the second song, he had already changed from audition to 'okay, can you play in this key?' He was already developing his program," Washtub said. He told the director he owned a tux, but they wanted him to wear his usual performing clothes including a cowboy hat and a vest. The orchestra backed him when he was doing solos, and he backed the orchestra in the role of a bassist. He has also performed at Lincoln Center in New York City.

Jerry has written a book, *Washtub Jerry: It Takes Pluck!* The book is described as "an illustrated guide to building and playing a washtub bass, plus many anecdotes." He has published three other books and was named the instrumentalist of the year in 1999 by the Western Music Association.

He performs with many other musicians including Glenn Moreland, Sid Hausman, Bill Chappell,

and Bruce Newman, and other bands in the Big Bend. He has recorded four CDs.

Bake Turner

Bake Turner was a presenter at the sessions "Pickin' and Grinnin'" and "Cowboys and Critters." When we met him a few months earlier, we interviewed him and Treva Watson, whom Bake introduces as his sweetheart.

Born in Alpine, Bake is a very popular guitarist. He has returned to Alpine in retirement and has three sisters who still live in the area. But before he pursued a full-time career in music, he had a career in professional football for nine years. Bake left Alpine to play football for Texas Tech, and after graduation he was drafted to play for the NFL's Baltimore Colts. "So I played a year with Johnny Unitas, Lenny Moore, and Raymond Berry. I played wide receiver, and then Coach Ewbank was fired. He went to the Jets in the AFL, and he asked me if I would go with him. It was all right with me if I could play," Bake said. "We spent a long time with the Jets in New York." Bake played in Super Bowl III in 1970 with Joe Namath, helping the Jets to victory.

During his seven years with the AFL Jets, Bake began filming commercials and appearing on television shows such as *The Tonight Show Starring Johnny Carson* and *The Ed Sullivan Show*. After the Super Bowl win, offers came in for national television commercials. A commercial for Score hair cream featured Bake, Don Maynard, Jim Turner, and Matt Snell, The Four Jets, singing a cover of the Johnny Nash song "Hold Me Tight." He wrote the final line of the jingle for Score aftershave: "Score if you're gonna play," a line that paid him $5,000. Bake played the DQ Dude for Dairy Queen for a year. "We did a commercial for Rango aftershave. I rode a horse on a mountain in the Big Bend and this girl was chasing me," Bake said. "I made more from commercials than from football."

He was also recording music during this time, songs such as "Violation" and "Is Anybody Going to

Bake Turner.

San Antone?" Bake still plays the 1965 Gibson guitar he bought in 1975.

After he retired from football, he moved to Dallas. "I raised my son in Dallas. Played a little there but mostly built houses. Then, I found myself alone so I came back to Alpine and fortunately, Treva was here," he said. Originally, he wanted to live in the Hill Country, so he lived in Fredericksburg for a while. "The parcels of land big enough for what I did, the mini ranches, were several hundred thousand dollars. I'd been paying twenty thousand in Dallas, so I came to Alpine," Bake explained. He began building on the more affordable lots in Alpine.

Bake only plays the guitar. "I've dabbled with harmonicas and I would love to play a fiddle, but I don't have time and I can't stand the screeching," he said. He keeps busy with gigs in Alpine and other places in Texas. "For instance, I went and played an anniversary in Lubbock. That's where I went to school. Some of my old friends are having sixtieth anniversaries. I go up there and play for those things. I don't like to travel much anymore because I can get all the music I want here," Bake said. He also participates in the American Legion open mike night, a weekly event in Alpine. Everyone sings along to old favorites such as "Cielito Lindo." Bake performs alone, although when he was younger, he performed with his sisters. "They were perfect harmony, but then they got busy with kids and grandkids, so I started being alone and I found this little computer about the size of a cigarette case with a foot pedal. It gives me three-part harmony when I call for it. So, when I sing George Strait and when it comes to his harmony parts, all those backup singers, it's just like it," Bake said. He also performs for the Trappings of Texas annual event and at the Gathering.

He writes songs, mainly humorous tunes that are known in the area, and sings Willie Nelson, Merle Haggard, Waylon Jennings, and the Eagles. He and Treva are considering retiring again from yet another career so they can travel.

Bake Turner and Treva Watson.

John Davis, Fort Davis, Texas.

John Davis

John Davis performed as a vocalist in the sessions "Saturday Night," "Shank of the Evenin'," "A Cowgirl and Her Heroes," "Pickin' and Grinnin'," and "Camp Coffee." He and his wife, Kayleen, own Limpia Creek Hat Company in Fort Davis.

John is originally from the Texas Panhandle and grew up on the ranches there. When he was six years old, he would accompany his mother and grandmother, bringing lunch to his grandfather's haying crew. "They'd cook all morning and put it in an old station wagon and go to the field where the crew was working. I'd listen to the radio and the guys would tease me and they'd want to know what I'd heard on the radio that day, so I'd sing them a song. They thought that was really funny," John said. He was able to hear a jingle on the radio and then sing it. He was twelve when his grandfather bought him his first guitar. "He bought it from a guy who won it at a poker game. There were several guys in town that would help you learn chords. I never was a very good guitar player. Just enough to accompany myself," he said. "At that time in the Panhandle there were talent shows, called hootenannies. All the little towns in the area had them, and anyone who had some sort of talent— dancers, singers, ventriloquists, and comedians—were welcome to perform." John's parents began taking him to these events.

"One of my mentors lived in that part of the world for years, he was a former Texas Playboy. His name was Frankie McWhorter. I sang with his band off and on, numerous times over the years. I got a lot of experience and learned a lot from him," John said. "I went to college and then decided I was going to be the next big singing sensation and that panned out real well," John laughed. He did sing in New York for an association at the Waldorf hotel.

That was in the mid-1970s. He continued singing with bands until he married Kayleen and started a family. He now sings at a lot of funerals and weddings and continues to perform with the local musicians

in Fort Davis and Alpine when he is called to sing at an event. Mainly, he is a solo vocalist. He finds that, unfortunately, he sings at a lot of funerals. "I've sung in church all my life; a lot of times when they ask me to sing they'll say, 'I don't know what we're going to do. We don't have a piano player or whatever.' I tell them, 'I don't need music. I just sing a cappella.' I do lots of gospel songs. I sing a number of songs in Spanish because a lot of the folks appreciate that, seeing an old, bald-headed white guy singing in Spanish. I try to do a wider variety of music," John said.

He also plays Texas swing and old honky-tonk music. His favorite singers are George Beverly Shea,

who sang on the Billy Graham crusades; Patsy Cline; and David Phelps, who sings with the Gaither Vocal Band.

He agrees with Don Cadden that the old western music is not being played by many younger musicians, the same membership the Gathering has been trying to recruit. The ranching way of life has changed as well, along with the times. "This is not the entertainment, the weekly entertainment anymore. The old-time cowboys didn't go to town. They didn't have all this other stuff bothering them. They played at home. The ranches have changed. Everything has changed so those young folks are not getting an opportunity to really play and learn that kind of old music," he said.

John worked on ranches for forty years, from northeastern New Mexico to the US-Mexico border and the Fulton Quien Sabe Ranch in the Texas Panhandle. Thirty years ago, a job at the Long X Ranch at Kent brought him to the Big Bend area, and he also worked at McCoy Land & Cattle in the Davis Mountains. John and Kayleen raised their children in the ranching way of life. "There was work to do and chores to do. There was all kinds of things for them to do, and not necessarily like there are now. We might have had a little bit of television but that was just if you could get the antenna just right," he said. Now his grandchildren, who live in Midland, come to visit in Fort Davis. "I try to make sure when the grandkids are here that they've got a little rope to try to rope a buck head or we will throw the football, the basketball. It's not really politically correct, but I got them a BB gun and we shoot the targets."

After a life of ranching, he became a custom hatmaker and moved into town, although he would still prefer to live outside Fort Davis. He began working at Limpia Creek Hat Company as a trainee. When the owner moved to Houston, taking the business with him, John returned to ranching, and then eight years later he bought the failing business back. John's hats are custom made from natural materials. "I don't put any powders or cosmetics on them. You don't know

if that material came from a colder climate, or a drier climate, or a wetter climate that year. It's either beaver or a blend of beaver and rabbit. So all of that material is different, but I'm going to spend a week, ten days, anyway. Some of them, you know, you think you're never going to get them finished because they're just not ready to finish. You never know how long it's going to take. It takes too long, really. I wish there was some way to speed it up, but it's like everything else. I could speed it up but then I probably wouldn't have much business," John said. His hats have been ordered from as far away as France, Australia, and Holland. In the United States, customers from states including Texas, Oklahoma, New Mexico, Colorado, and Louisiana order hats from the Limpia Creek Hat Company.

Jim Wilson

Jim Wilson, a singer and guitar player, performed at the Gathering sessions "Head 'em Up, Move 'em Out," "Saddling Up Time," "Triple Trouble," and "Swift Justice." He writes poetry and songs and entertains at other Cowboy Poetry Gatherings and western music festivals across the country.

Jim was born in Austin and raised in San Antonio. He retired after thirty years in law enforcement and then was elected sheriff of Crockett County. Jim has worked on ranches since his teens in addition to team roping and working rodeos. His early musical influence was his father singing "The Streets of Laredo" and "Leaving Cheyenne," classic old cowboy songs.

While he attended Texas Christian University in the 1960s, he played folk and country music but returned to cowboy music twenty years later. In 2003, Jim's record *Border Bravo* won Best Traditional Album from the Western Music Association. He served as vice president of the Western Music Association and remains active in the organization.

He also writes features and columns for gun magazines such as *Guns & Ammo*, *Handloader*,

Jim Wilson.

and *Shooting Times* as handgun editor and is currently writing the column "Straight Talk" for NRA Publications in their magazine *Shooting Illustrated*. In addition, he frequently appears on the Outdoor Channel and is a regular on the NRA's *American Guardian* television show.

Jim voices the same concerns about the preservation of traditional music by a new generation. "The modern communications has affected that. Everybody can hear everybody else now and so you've got a lot of copying going on. The older bands, like the bands down in Presidio, there was an isolation back in those days. So, they worked up their own style. There's the style of music that they liked and they enjoyed playing because they weren't trying to copy anyone else," he explained. "We see the same thing in the old cowboy poetry. Badger Clark, those kinds of early poets were out on the ranches by themselves, and they started writing poetry in the evenings. No television, probably no radio. Their style developed unaffected by what's going on in Nashville or Los Angeles."

Jim sees a difference in the music he performs in Marfa. Since Marfa has established its reputation as an artists' town, tourists who come to Marfa expect a unique experience that also includes music. Some musicians have named Marfa "Taos South." When Jim performed at Cibolo Ranch, near Presidio, for a group of tourists from London, they wanted to hear traditional cowboy music. "Most of us that play music around here play a variety of styles. I play cowboy music, I play folk, old-time country and I'll tend to kind of blend those in. An audience that likes a cowboy song like something written by Ian Tyson, they'll enjoy a Guy Clark song," he said. He also performs some songs from Mexico. His favorites are "Cielito Lindo," the revolutionary song "Adelita," and "Jalisco No Te Rajes," depending on his audience.

He has a philosophy about the relationship between performer and audience. "Any performance is a dialogue, and I think that's critical to keep in mind. If I'm up dancing the *Nutcracker Suite*, that's really a dialogue between me and the audience. Your audience will tell you, maybe not verbally, but you'll get an idea from your audience what they would like to hear," he explained. "Your job is to entertain them, not impress them. Let them have this little escape and release for a little while and enjoy themselves, escaping from whatever else is going on in their life. I think you have to know a variety of music in order to accomplish that."

Glenn Moreland

Glenn Moreland was also a performer at the Gathering at the sessions "Horseman Philosophy," "Embarrassing Moments," and "Cowboys, Horses, and Dogs." In addition to singing and playing the guitar and sometimes the fiddle, he owns and operates a chuck wagon, catering events with his wife, Patty.

Glenn was born in Manchaca, Texas, ten miles southwest of Austin. He began his musical career learning the guitar during high school when he was unable to work one summer. Subsequently, he was stepped on by a bull and faced a period of convalescence. Both times, his mother sent him to town to take guitar lessons. "I mostly play western music, cowboy music, so it was on Labor Day out at Oak Hill, Texas, they had a Labor Day roping. There was a man named John Birch and he would come and rope. He would be out behind the chutes playing a guitar and singing these old cowboy songs, playing the fiddle, playing the mandolin, and that just blew my mind away, so I went and found a fiddle and I was playing a guitar, but I started learning the old cowboy songs and have been playing them ever since," Glenn said.

He used to play with the well-known musician Washtub Jerry, for Elderhostel. That audience appreciated old western music, such as Roy Rogers and the Sons of the Pioneers. "Western songs are mostly about horses, the country, the scenery, romantic-type songs. Western romantic. The country songs are just beer drinking, losing your wife and car wrecks," Glenn said. He believes there is no country-western, that

Glenn Moreland.

the western was taken out of country-western when Tex Ritter died.

He moved to El Paso for a year, worked in a feed-lot, and then moved with his wife back to the Big Bend. They bought the Drugstore in Fort Davis, which is not an actual drugstore but an ice cream parlor and breakfast and lunch restaurant on the main street. "We didn't have a lick of business sense but we assumed the note and ran it for about five years until the gas crisis in the seventies, when the tourist trade dropped off, and we finally got out from under that. Her mother had a ranch at the time and I'd work at the ranch one day and work at the Drugstore the next. You could say I was an official drugstore cowboy," Glenn laughed.

Glenn eventually came to the Big Bend because his wife, Patty, was raised there, as her mother was raised in Marfa. When they graduated from college, Glenn had a degree in agricultural education but couldn't find a teaching job. The job he did land was testing for brucellosis in Fort Bend County near Houston. Patty had a job teaching in El Paso, making it very hard for the newlyweds. Glenn began working on collecting, restoring, and building wagons. "When I was a cow inspector, I got a chuck wagon and running gear that I bought down there forty-something years ago," Glenn said. When chuck wagon competitions began in the area, Glenn partnered with a cook and began competing. He realized that the chuck wagon was ideal for catering. Sometimes he caters two events a month, but then he may not have another booking for six months.

Glenn took us to the large outbuilding next to his house where he keeps the wagons that are undergoing restoration and the large wagon he takes to events. It is an authentic chuck wagon with meticulous attention to authenticity.

Glenn had a group called Fiddle Grass that played with Washtub Jerry, with whom he has performed for forty years and still plays events in the area. When they changed the name to Fiddle West, they were playing western music and bluegrass. The four-person group, which included two women, one a teacher and one

a banker, was reduced to only two people when the women moved away. Glenn played the fiddle and Jerry would play the ukulele and the washtub.

Attending the Gathering strengthens the commitment to preserve the classic western music of Roy Rogers, the Sons of the Pioneers, Hopalong Cassidy, Gene Autry, Bob Wills, Tex Ritter, and groups that predate those performers. It is an oral history preserved through both old and current poetry, song, and music. Although the ranching life has changed along with the times, the traditions of the West live on at the Alpine Cowboy Poetry Gathering.

The Alpine Cowboy Poetry Gathering of 2019 was the last of that name. However, the Lone Star Cowboy Poetry Gathering formed after the announcement of the end of the Alpine Gathering. The organization plans to continue the tradition and announced a meeting in February 2020. Many of the participants and performers from the long-standing Alpine Cowboy Poetry Gathering intend to gather again in Alpine to perform and keep the traditions alive.

9

The Bands

LOW POPULATION DENSITY and long hauls between gigs make it hard for a big group to make much money playing music in the Big Bend. Most of the ensembles that stay together for any length of time tend to number no more than four. But the groups that do hang in for any period of time typically develop their own unique followings. And, like everything else in this part of the country, they each tend to develop unique approaches and a healthy sense of humor, with a side helping of persistence, in order to keep going.

Just Us Girls (JUGS)

Chris Müller, Shanna Cowell, Evie Dorsey, Christine Baker, and Charlotte Teer Egerton started Just Us Girls, the only all-woman band in the Big Bend, in the 1990s. Shanna Cowell remembers when they named the band. "It was a joke, you know, because we were all flat chested. We came up with Just Us Girls. 'Hey, that's a great name!' Then somebody said, 'Hey, J-U-G-S, jugs.' And we just cracked up." The other four members began playing together in 1992 and Shanna joined them from 1993 until 1996. At that point, Charlotte moved to Idaho, Evie moved to Dallas, and Shanna went to school in Austin.

Predictably, they had difficulty breaking into the male-dominated music scene of the time. "There were the boys. The boys kind of controlled the music scene. They'd have a gig and supposedly it would be a 'come on and play with us and jam,' except that they really didn't mean the girls. You know what I mean," said Chris Müller.

"We deserved time at the mike, but we were never asked onstage. One time all five of us had our instruments but were never called up," said Evie.

"The boys' club were brats," Charlotte said. "Two and a half hours waiting to play and we were never called up."

Shanna, as a drummer, had a slightly different experience. "Part of the reason we had an all-woman band was because the guys wouldn't let us play with them. I played with the guys because I was a rhythm player. They were happy to have me in there playing unobtrusive stuff so that they could shine on whatever they were doing. So I was a low-key bass player, low-key drummer that they could have walk in on the gigs and it was fine. The other girls were singer-songwriters and the

Chris Müller.

Shanna Cowell.

Close-up of Shanna Cowell's washboard instrument, made by the late Uh Clem of Terlingua.

the area, she fell in love with the scenery and bought twenty acres of land to homestead, hauling water and building a home from scratch. Although now she also has a home in Silver City, New Mexico, she spends most of the year in the Big Bend. She is the owner of the store Christine's World in Lajitas.

She still performs in Terlingua by sitting in with other musicians. Christine sings and plays the guitar and flute. "Christine did avant garde jazz, blues, that was what she was into," said Shanna. Charlotte, Shanna, and Christine are all classically trained; Shanna concentrated more on theory and composition and Christine was more performance oriented, Shanna explained. They play a wide variety of music.

Evie Dorsey was born in Texarkana, Texas, and went to school at Southern Methodist University, graduating with a degree in theater. She is a talented singer, songwriter, and musician and toured with Townes Van Zandt in the late 1960s and early 1970s. She moved to the Big Bend in 1990, after living there from 1985 to 1986. She was familiar with the area from leading tours there from 1983 to 1992. "Big Bend is the area that matches my soul, it inspires me," Evie said.

She moved to Dallas in the mid-1990s and taught at the Saint Alcuin School as a Montessori teacher, but she plans to retire soon. She has fond memories of the group: "We were five individual, independent women. The great gift of Just Us Girls was that it empowered us to perform our music, bringing together this disparate group, we ended up inspiring women to express themselves in song," Evie said.

Chris credits Evie for starting the group: "Evie says, 'I want to make a band. I want to put a band together of girls.' She started with me. I was the first one and she talked me into it. I had no idea how big a band this would be or anything. We didn't say to these women, 'We're putting a band together,' but we said, 'Let's see about jamming with them,' and we'd jam with some different people. But it was girls, it was women. It was not men," she said. Evie brought in Christine Baker and her flute. Soon she was also playing the

guys were not interested in being upstaged by another woman songwriter-singer in the band," she explained.

Christine also remembers the early days of JUGS: "They had a pretty good little music scene and decent pickers. They would let Shanna play with them because she played the drums. We'd go to a gig and they'd say to come sit in, we'd go and they'd never call us up there or anything like that, so we just formed our own group."

Christine Baker came to live in Terlingua by learning about it during a geology course at the University of North Texas in Denton. When she came to see guitar and singing. "She has a voice like velvet, an amazing voice. Later, Christine shared her original songs and her harmonies, and we performed what she wrote," said Chris. Evie remembers the group booking gigs outside Terlingua, in Marfa, at the Hallie Stillwell Ranch, and at celebrations on both sides of the border.

Originally from Michigan, Chris moved to Houston in 1978. "I'd been an actress; I'd been in theater. I had visited Houston and I loved the music scene at that time. So I moved there to be part of that and I got to be a professional musician in Houston during that time because I had stage presence. So it got me through the fact that I didn't know much about playing the guitar," Chris said. She played at Fitzgerald's and Anderson Fair and other musical venues in Houston, which became increasingly difficult because she was a solo act and bands were more popular, so she decided to move to Austin in 1982. "Houston got crazier. People were shooting each other over fender benders. It was time to get out of Dodge. So I moved to Austin, but the Austin music scene was really hard. Good musicians were a dime a dozen. Excellent musicians, a quarter a dozen. I wasn't an excellent musician. I had a good voice, but I wasn't a great musician," she explained.

Chris's friend Nancy Clifford introduced her to the Big Bend. After another visit, Chris decided to move there. It was a chance to get away from all the urban problems. When she moved in the late 1980s, she began playing with Charlotte. "I moved to Terlingua and when I was there I met a musical friend, Charlotte Teer, and she and I started playing music together. She plays viola and she sang these amazing harmonies, and so we ended up being this little duo, Chris and Charlotte. We played for years and years." Chris brought Charlotte into the group and Evie brought Christine. "Then Evie brought in Shanna and called Shanna our heartbeat," Chris said. In addition to playing the drums, Shanna also played what Chris calls the rhythm jig, which is a washboard, and the tambourine. "At one time the biggest bands and biggest draws were us and the Pinche Gringos," Chris said.

Christine Baker.

She moved to Alpine and worked for Big Canyon Television, a satellite television business. "I had a guy come in one day who saw me and said, 'Didn't you used to be a musician?' Well, at the time it broke my heart because I hadn't given it up yet, mentally, but after I got sick, I had to." It was fortunate she had access to medical care because Chris had to have several brain surgeries. "I got something called normal pressure hydrocephalus. I almost died. And in the meantime, I also broke my hip, so I'm in a different place now. If I had been in Terlingua when that happened, I'd be dead. It changed my life, and afterward, I had time to do music since I didn't go back to work. This happened eight years ago, but I didn't care about music that much anymore," she said.

She did one performance after the surgery, reuniting with Ted Arbogast of Los Pinche Gringos. Ted played guitar and Evie sang. "I sang torchy tunes; we did that for years and dressed up. I pretended I was Peggy Lee because I can sing 'Fever,' I can belt it. I went down and did one of those after my illness. People came out just to see if I could sing and I could, but I would cry. I still do sometimes, tears run down my face when I'm singing and it's something that I don't feel comfortable about so I stopped gigging," Chris explained.

Shanna Cowell moved to Alpine at the age of eight. Her two older brothers, Stephen and Jeff, were born there, but the family moved to Euless, Texas, and her brothers went to elementary school in Euless. Shanna's early musical influences were her parents. "My mother got me started on piano when I was eight and my dad taught me my first song on piano and on guitar when I was little. My parents encouraged us in music from when we were little kids," she said.

Growing up in Alpine, she listened to KVLF, first mostly big band music, then country-western. "I played big band in jazz bands and in school, I played brass. I played euphonium in school, which is a brass instrument. First I played piano, a little bit of guitar, and then I got into the euphonium, then I started playing more rock and roll instruments, and the drums," Shanna said. She brings out what appears to be a modified washboard, invented by her late friend Clem Rothelle, known as "Uh Clem" of Terlingua, nicknamed after a character on the Firesign Theatre, adding expertise on yet another instrument.

Shanna lived in Austin for several years, playing drums for a punk rock band. "You can't get paid in Austin because anybody and everybody wants to be a star and anybody and everybody will play for nothing. When I was there last, the clubs would hire people to play that would just play for tips or play for nothing," Shanna said. When she moved to Terlingua in the early 1990s, the music scene was all local talent, playing mostly for fun or for benefits. "It was a lot of really spontaneous fun, wonderful music, all acoustic," she said.

When she joined JUGS they played an eclectic selection of music. "We had probably twenty-five to thirty percent that was original; Evie was more old-timey. She would play Stephen Foster, 'Saint James Infirmary,' 'Buffalo Gals.' Chris Müller had been a solo artist in Houston and played just singer-songwriter solo stuff for a long time. So she was bringing in Guy Clark or those Texana guys, Americana, that kind of work," Shanna said. "They played the Austin-type music and Texas Americana. Christine Baker was more the California folk hippie girl. She was playing Buffy Sainte-Marie or Joni Mitchell, James Taylor. So we had kind of a mix but there were things that overlapped and had roots of each other in them." After the band scattered in 1997, Shanna returned to Terlingua in 2001, opening an acupuncture clinic. She moved back to Alpine in 2005. She owns the White Crane Acupuncture Clinic, also specializing in Chinese medicine.

Shanna still enjoys performing occasionally with the other three members who still get together. "I love them all. It was great, one-on-one with each of them, but when they all came together there were sparks, that's what made the music so amazing," she said.

Charlotte lives in Mackay, Idaho, from June to November each year, then in the Big Bend from December to May. She was born in Odessa and fell in love with the Big Bend at the age of four on a family vacation. "I knew I would live there. Odessa is real flat. If you want to expand your horizons, get in the bed of a pickup and stand up, you can see real far," she said.

When Charlotte moved to Terlingua in the late 1980s, she began performing with Chris Müller. Christine began playing viola and cello and singing with Chris in the early 1990s, and then Evie joined the group, then Shanna. Charlotte worked in the hotel in Lajitas and was a horseback guide. She found that she missed having a wide selection of groceries. "While living in Lajitas, your choice back then in fruits and vegetables were bananas and onions and an occasional orange," she said. Since then, with the increase in population, that is not as much of a problem.

The most recent appearance of the now four-member JUGS was New Year's Day on the iconic Front Porch of the Terlingua Trading Company for the Black-Eyed Pea-Off fundraiser, a tradition since 1990 benefiting the Last Minute Low Budget Productions company.

Evie sums up their experience: "Greatness comes when we stay away from 'I' or 'me.' There is a thing that happens to us; our energy is more than the five of us."

Craig Carter and the Spur of the Moment Band

Craig Carter and his Spur of the Moment band, with Zack Casey on lead guitar, Charlie Thomas on drums, Yadon Hardaway on bass, and Craig on acoustic guitar and lead vocals, played for the dance on the last night of the Gathering at the Alpine Civic Center. When we told Don Cadden we interviewed Craig, he wanted to tell us that Craig is a key figure at the Gathering. "I don't know if he told you this or not, but I'm going to tell you. Craig has been at this Gathering since the beginning and he's very much a part of it because of his ranching heritage. He's the music guy out here in terms of dances," Don said. "Craig has been to Europe over sixty times and he still goes back to Switzerland. Craig was, I would say, the George Strait of Switzerland. He could have moved over there and been a hero. They loved him. Craig's a really good horseman and he's really good with people." Craig was in the sessions "We Pointed 'em North" and "Nighthawkin.'"

Craig Carter is a handsome man with piercing blue eyes. When we met him for the second time on his ranch south of Marathon, he was dressed in his leather chaps and cowboy hat and had his horse Cisco with him. He was the perfect image of a cowboy in a western movie, which is fitting since he has appeared in movies and television commercials for Dr Pepper, Budweiser, Marlboro, the Boot Barn, and Chevrolet. We toured his ranch in his rough-terrain Polaris and it was a scene of remote, breathtaking beauty. His is a working ranch and he is truly in his element there.

"Through music I started working in film, and early on I was trying to be in front of the camera. I was working all over: Nashville, Houston . . . anywhere I would spend any length of time on a job I would set up acting lessons. I went out and met with some agents and got a commercial theatrical agent," he said. Craig had his "biggest" small part in the movie *The Hi-Lo Country*. "It was loaded up with stars and not a bad movie, but I just had a small role. I would go to LA and I had friends there in the entertainment industry, and I'd get day work, whether it would be wrangling animals or livestock—I grew up with horses—or work as a stunt driver in a car," Craig said.

Marathon is his home. "I was raised right here. On my mom's side of the family, we're from the Marathon area for a hundred years. And we don't say 'Mar-a-THON'; if you're from here, it's 'Mar-a-thin,'" he said. He was raised on ranches in the area. His parents met in Big Bend National Park, where his mother worked for the park concessions. "My dad worked for the horse outfit. He went on to manage it. He was from East Texas. He came out here because of Sul Ross. He fell in love with the country and then fell in love with Mom. A large part of my life was actually in the Chisos Basin," he explained. His family owned and operated the Chisos Remuda and the horse rides there. His father was also a musician. "My dad played music and had a good voice. He was the kind of person that whatever he tried to tackle, he could tackle," he said. Craig began playing the guitar at fifteen and had a small band by sixteen. He has been writing songs since then.

It was through his film work that he met his wife, Shannon, when they worked together on a PBS show called *Texas Ranch House* that was filmed on a ranch

Craig Carter.

thirty miles outside Alpine. "We worked together for four or five months. It was a pretty big show. And I wouldn't let her go home. She worked until we had a child, our daughter Sadie, and I would follow her around and support her, help her. I would say that it's tough out here, especially on females. You know, I have a sister that was raised here and to me, it's harder on the girls than it is the boys," he said. "It's hard enough on anybody to make a living, but it's the remoteness. Shannon loves it, she's adapted. She's from Huntington Beach. Grew up a little bit in Idaho. We were almost camping out on that job. It was pretty rough conditions. Everything turns into a job. We live on a ranch and there's always something to do."

His life of ranching led to the position of head wrangler or head animal trainer for movies and television productions. Craig's horse Cisco has appeared with him in the reality show *Arizona Cowboy* and acquired fans of his own. Craig's film and television credits include his job as a wrangler, also providing horses for such movies as *No Country for Old Men*, *True Grit*, *The Hunger Games*, and *Twelve Years a Slave*.

He and his family also tour Europe frequently, where Craig has a following. He categorizes his music as "border country," a description he heard of his music from Richard Fallon, a former owner of Railroad Blues in Alpine. "It's a Spanish-German cross. The German aspect of the Spanish music and influences, I got to see full circle. I spent sixty tours in Europe—in Switzerland, Austria, Germany— and the music there is so comparable to the Spanish music I grew up with and I love it. So, I sing in Spanish. I don't do much straight-up Mexican music. You don't know that I'm American when I speak Spanish. It's not like I'm a hundred percent anymore, but I used to be," he said. The Spur of the Moment band got their name because, depending on the gig, they may have a lead guitar and fiddle or they may have keyboards. "Growing up out here there's not a lot of musicians. I've been real fortunate, after growing up, Zack and Charlie and I have been together

Craig Carter and Cisco.

for over twenty years. I've known Yadon since second grade, right here," said Craig.

In addition to performing the songs he has written, many of which are well known in the Big Bend, Craig enjoys playing Willie Nelson, with about twenty of his songs in his repertoire. He also plays Merle Haggard, Johnny Duncan, and Bob Wills, and he worked with the Texas Tornados. "When I was younger I did not like Merle Haggard. My father did and so did my uncle. They'd get together and play music. In my midtwenties is when it hit me: What is wrong with me? And now, I'm such a huge fan. I mean, seldom do you hear a voice like his that needed less backup," he said.

Craig is a well-respected musician and rancher. His Spur of the Moment band is very popular in the Big Bend. At this last event of the Gathering, couples crowd the floor, two-stepping to his music, the "border country" style he loves.

Los Pinche Gringos

One of the most well-known and popular bands, in addition to Craig Carter's Spur of the Moment band, is Los Pinche Gringos from Terlingua. The members of the band are Mike Davidson on guitar and vocals, Laird Considine on bass and vocals, Ted Arbogast on guitar, keyboard, and vocals, and George Womack on drums.

Mike Davidson was born and raised in Sugar Land, Texas. After high school, he stayed in the Houston area until he visited the Big Bend in 1975 on his way to Wyoming, where he planned to move. "I wanted to go someplace where there were mountains and outdoor activities. I came out to visit the Big Bend for the first time in 1975 and I'm still here. I moved here permanently in '77," he said. Mike settled in Terlingua and cofounded Far Flung Adventures. "I came in with a pickup truck and a couple of old, used rafts, and just started plying our trade and didn't know that we were providing something that people would seek out. I had a few little connections and it started growing from there. In January of 1979, we had the cover story on *Southern Living* magazine. So, boom! We went from a crew of four to a crew of twelve overnight," Mike said. He raised a family in the Big Bend, and his children were born at home in Terlingua. He was most comfortable with a rural environment. When he was growing up, Sugarland had a population of three thousand, was relatively small, and still had open prairies nearby. Mike's parents took him and his two brothers camping in the national parks, so Mike always wanted to live near one.

He began his music experience with piano lessons at the age of nine and played trumpet in his junior high band. His parents played and his brothers started

out on trombone. His middle brother earned a degree in music education from North Texas State University (now the University of North Texas) and is now a band director. When that brother received a guitar for Christmas and was not interested in it at the time, Mike began playing it. He was twelve when he began playing, and he never quit.

When Mike moved to Terlingua he began playing in bands, starting with his brothers and some local musicians in a group called the Terlingua All Stars. Then he performed in a group with some river guides called the Rafters. It was when he joined Craig Carter, a singer-songwriter in Marathon and his band that he began performing frequently. "He was real active back then so I joined him as the bass player. We were probably working forty-five dates a year, almost every weekend. We did some tours in Switzerland. He had made contact with a musician in another country band in Switzerland. There's a country band! Many of these people were having to sing English phonetically because they did not know any English, so that was really interesting," Mike said. "Then Ted Arbogast, who is kind of our brilliant lead guitar player and all around musician, we played around campfires and stuff, found ourselves playing in Craig Carter's band."

At a celebrity benefit roping contest in Houston, Mike and Ted were performing in Craig Carter's Spur of the Moment band when their determination to learn Mexican songs to perform became a reality. "I'd always enjoyed listening to that music, as the rancheros and stuff were really light. Even if they're singing about massacres and people getting their heads cut off, it's nice melodies and everything. So we picked out some tunes to try to learn. My Spanish was pretty good back then, but think about the Rolling Stones songs. Who can understand what the hell they're saying, even if you know the language?" he said. "So we found a waiter at our restaurant from somewhere and we asked him if he would write down the words to the songs. We'd send him a list and he wrote them down and we started doing some of those." Back home,

Los Pinche Gringos, performing in Terlingua.

they found a seasonal park ranger from Panama, Ian Sanchez, who was also a singer and drummer. They started their band and learned a lot of Mexican songs. In the beginning, Mike sang harmony and was a backup singer. After rehearsing three nights a week for several months, they were ready to play in public. The name of their band turned out to be controversial, since "pinche" is a vulgar word in Mexico. "We're just a bunch of pinche gringos, so what the heck? But then there was a local lady that printed up the kind of weekly 'What's Happening in Terlingua' and they put it up at the post office and she heard that we were going to play at the Starlight Theatre. Well, what's your name? Well, Los Pinche Gringos. She was incensed as the arbiter of our social mores in Terlingua so she refused to print it and then we knew it! That's what we are!" said Mike. They encountered resistance to their name from people on both sides of the border. "The Mexican people didn't want to say our name and they didn't put up posters around town, but they showed up out of curiosity. Some people find it humorous and some people find it very offensive. To the older Hispanic community here it was very offensive. But to the Railroad Blues [crowd] it was like, yeah, put it on the big sign out there on the highway. What I've experienced is that they expect we'd kind of come and gone, 'Oh, these guys are going to try and play Mexican music.' They wouldn't say our name but they ended up dancing and it was just a fun community thing to kind of see happen," said Laird. They performed at Railroad Blues to packed houses and their popularity grew, as did their mix of music from both sides of the border. "There are two cultures here that live side by side and we had gringos and Mexicans all out on the floor dancing," Laird said.

Mike quickly points out that there is more than one meaning of the word "pinche." "It is a word in Castilian that refers to a scullery maid. As you can imagine, that's one of the worst jobs. You know, they're looked down on. Its connotation in Mexico has become a little bit deeper, whereas in Spain, it's maybe an archaic word but it refers to the lady that has to clean all the grease out of the pots in the restaurant. In Arizona they tend to use it as 'stingy.' It doesn't refer to the sexual act, but is like, f'ing gringos, you know?" he said.

"We've recently added a member who has to come from Austin to play; she plays saxophone, flute, and violin: a serious, full-time musician," Mike said. She teaches full time in addition to performing in Austin six nights a week. "She has private students who she teaches at her house, and she has a couple of schools that she goes in and does school stuff with. She's brought a level of enthusiasm back, because there's just another element to the sound and we all like it really well. We try to include her in on it," Mike said.

In addition to playing rock and roll, country, and their original songs, the Gringos play cumbias. "Cumbia is an interesting music form. Purportedly, this rhythm originated in Colombia, really a hotbed of this really good music. This cumbia has spread around through Latin America and Mexico. Sometimes it's infused with a little Afro-Caribe," Mike said. "It's something just fun to play. It's really light, happy music. Most of the lyrics are about going dancing and going to the beach. We do several cumbias about farmyard animals, which are kind of a double entendre. It's 'all my hens are red and your rooster is black. And all my little chickens come out black. Your rooster's in my henhouse.' It's really easy to dance to, everybody dances to cumbia."

When Mike first moved to the Big Bend, if there was a dance in Terlingua or Lajitas, it would draw people from all over the area since that was a major social event. Mike notes that for performances in a more urban setting, after dark was the time to drink and loosen up, when people would dance. But in West Texas, everyone is dancing from the first note.

Ted, Mike, and Laird all played for Craig Carter's band before they decided to start playing Mexican music. "No one was playing this music. I played blues, rock and roll, and country," Laird said. "I thought it wouldn't go anywhere, these white guys playing Mexican music."

In the Big Bend, people from both sides of the river like cumbias and rancheros, but also rock and roll and country. Los Pinche Gringos play classic country, usually not anything less than twenty years old. "Music is kind of a language so I like to say anybody can play a song they know. Nowadays with this digital stuff Ted has on his mike, he's got his little phone and he dials it in and knows if he needs to remind us of the words or if we want to learn a new song. We can kind of cater to an audience. If people don't seem to be responding really well, maybe they're not really liking this Mexican music, so we'll do some Merle Haggard or George Jones, the classics," he said. The Gringos also play medleys, blending cumbias with Beatles songs or Merle Haggard, keeping the beat and the dancers on the floor.

The three original members of the Pinche Gringos—Mike, Laird, and Ted—have been playing together for twenty-five years. In that time, they have had eight drummers, two of them Juilliard trained. Their current drummer, George Womack, is retired from the Houston Symphony.

After years as a river guide, Mike now leads interpretative historical and geological tours of the Big Bend through the Big Bend Texas Travel Company. The tours draw clients both nationally and internationally and start from Marathon, Terlingua, Lajitas, the Chisos Mountains Lodge, and Alpine.

Laird Considine sings and plays the bass guitar, not only with the Gringos but also with other bands, and performs solo and in a trio. He grew up in Midland but came from Austin to the Big Bend. "I felt like this was home. I had a long relationship with this area since the early seventies. I remember Craig Carter leading a horse tour when he was about twelve years old," Laird said. Ironically, he became the lead bass player for Craig's band when he moved to the Big Bend.

Laird met Ted Arbogast in Arizona and played with Ted's brother. When he moved to Austin a year later, he contacted Ted, who had bought forty acres near Terlingua. Laird decided to visit Ted and moved there a year later. He recorded a CD in Ted's studio, finding when he moved to Terlingua that there was a vibrant and active music scene. "There was an incredible local scene. Austin was supposed to be the music capital of Texas, but it is here. In a week I had paying gigs, and not in Austin," he said. He performed in a group called Dr. Fun and the Flying Javelinas playing Texas swing, as well as with other groups.

Bands who come to Terlingua have also been influenced by the binational music played there. Laird observes that more conjunto and norteño are being played by outside bands. Ted believes Joe King Carrasco was the first to bring this music from outside Terlingua to be performed there. Ted calls it "cumbia style for gringos."

The band still performs at regular gigs such as the Chili Cookoff, the Ride 4 Trails rally and benefit, and the West Texas Judges and Commissioners Annual Meeting. Other gigs throughout the Big Bend include ranch parties and events not in bars, where the gigs run late. They play twelve to fifteen times a year, but the Gringos don't play as often now since they are getting older. "Maybe we should change our names to Los Pinche Viejos," Laird laughs.

Ted Arbogast is from the Tucson–southern Arizona area, where he was born and raised and earned an IT degree. He moved to Austin to work. "I enjoyed a time at the Kerrville Folk Festival where I jammed with some people who became dear friends who live in Terlingua, Jack and Alice Knight. Alice is a very prolific songwriter, and I have recorded and produced at least eleven albums with her," Ted said.

After Ted's work in Austin was done in 1990, he packed up his trailer and his dog and moved to the Big Bend. Ted began performing shortly thereafter with Mike Davidson. "We lamented the lack of any kind of dance band in the area, and we both loved Mexican music. One gig with Craig, we sidemen pulled out 'Luis Pulido,' a popular corrido, and the energy was big! Seems everybody in Texas relates at some level to Mexican ranchera music," he said. Laird Considine,

Ted Arbogast.

whom Ted describes as a "naturalist and able boat-man and bass man," came out from Austin to be in the newly formed band. "We hunted up our first drum-mer, Ian Sanchez, a boatman from Panama, rehearsed a week or two, and started playing the clubs in south county. We've been through around ten drummers, but the core three ain't going nowhere," he said.

Ted also has a recording studio, Studio Butte, which he has had since 1995, but he began recording and producing in Tucson in 1978. "The first CD out of [Studio Butte] was Laird's *Ghost Tones*. Since then about seventy-five albums have come out of there and still do, including rock, country, Mexican, metal, folk bands, and the Pinche Gringos," Ted said.

Since 1990, Ted has seen changes in the music scene in the Big Bend, particularly in Terlingua, where most of the activity revolved around three porches: the Study Butte Store, the Lajitas Trading Post, and the Ghost Town. There was one bar, La Kiva. The musicians would informally gather to jam.

"Everything, from my perspective, revolved around these porches. Memes were created, shared, tossed, emboldened; friendships cemented, cast aside; songs created on the fly or brought down from the hinterlands; dancers danced, babies were made. A porch never closes, unlike a bar. The village econ-omy was and still is based on tourism and I submit that these porches could be almost as big a tourist draw as river running and backcountry jeeps. Most tourists know that to understand a region, it's good to listen to its music. Musicians would just start playing, and within an hour the crowd would find us," Ted explained.

Now, decades later, there is a much larger population, but only one porch, four bars, and many more musicians. "Music here has always come from some intrepid soul strumming a guitar by some campfire and getting the message just right, then coming to the porch and singing, or getting to the studio to record, or debuting it at a club. That has not changed, but the stars and coyotes got to hear it first," Ted said.

Computers have been Ted's career, and he has worked at the Terlingua school district for the last twenty-three years. He is also the director of the Big Bend High School Roadrunner Band.

Ted also pays tribute to his early days as a musician in the Big Bend. "I want to acknowledge my early jamming buddies and musical gurus, Charlie Maxwell and Doug Davis. Doug and I played duo around Terlingua in the nineties. We lost Doug some time back. Charlie and I still make really fine music. Playing with Doug was like being in the Bob Wills band, and playing with Charlie can't really be categorized, you just have to hear it, really. Desert music goes to a Pink Floyd concert?"

The Doodlin' Hogwallops

The core members of the Doodlin' Hogwallops are Neil Trammell, Chris McWilliams, and Todd Elrod. They met as students at Sul Ross State University.

Neil grew up south of Fort Worth in Godley, Texas, and went to Trinity University in San Antonio, playing football. "I played a lot of music. In fact, my freshman roommate was Will Dupuy, who ended up being a founding member of the South Austin Jug Band. Austin just dedicated a day to him because of his donation to kids' music in Austin. He's Mr. Will. He's huge. We were freshman roommates. Kind of like the

Lyle Lovett / Robert Earl Keen story. We just haven't reached their level of success by any means," said Neil.

When Neil's grades weren't high enough to continue at Trinity, he went home and attended community college to raise his GPA. The head football coach from Sul Ross came to town. "My old coach from high school was nice enough to say, 'This kid needs a second chance.' I loaded up with my dad on a Tuesday and we drove to Alpine. Came in, met the head coach, went and applied for school, had a dorm, had my classes scheduled, it all took about fifteen minutes. I thought, 'This is the place for me!'" Neil explained. "I went home the first summer and I worked and I came back to school. But I stayed that second summer and then that third summer . . . and the rain would come in across Sunny Glen, and believe it or not, I did go to the library. You could watch it from the library up there and it would just cover the valley. I just fell in love with it. Since then, I've worked hard to figure out how to make my living here. Whatever I have to do. Music became a part of that early on, like, '03 or '04."

Neil began playing a very rudimentary guitar that he remembers as a sort of fake Ovation with a plastic back. "You could write a song, flip it over, and eat cereal out of it," Neil laughs. His uncle Larry put new strings on it and taught Neil the chords to the Jerry Jeff Walker song "Jaded Lover" and the Robert Earl Keen song "Merry Christmas to the Family." He brought those two songs to Trinity. "I'd get up at six and I'd play those two songs for a couple of hours before I went to class. My roommates, my suitemates, all my neighbors hated me because I only knew two songs, but that was where it started. Then, the second semester I met Will and he was playing bass with Rodney Haydon at the time. They were always playing in Bandera, opening up for people. Robert Earl Keen's wife was managing Rodney Haydon's career at that point. I got to meet Chris LeDoux, Dell Watson, everybody that was sort of big in the world played in Bandera at the Cabaret. They were the opening band

The Doodlin' Hogwallops. *Left to right*: Todd Elrod, Neil Trammell, Chris McWilliams.

Neil Trammell.

so I would go carry a bass amp and get in free and just got immersed in all the music," he said.

When Neil was fifteen he listened to the Mike Crow show on 96.3 KSCS out of Dallas every Sunday night. Crow featured only Texas artists and honky-tonk music from performers such as Ray Wylie Hubbard, Robert Earl Keen, Tommy Albertson, and Billy Joe Shaver. Although Neil did not play the guitar until he was eighteen, he was already writing poetry that he believed could be turned into song lyrics.

In Alpine he began performing with Todd Elrod in such venues as the Crystal, the Buffalo Rose, and a monthly gig at the Gage Hotel in Marathon for $200, which covered their rent of $190. They also performed with the band Impotent Horny Toads. Some of those musicians still perform. "Basically, there was a heavy metal band called Demon Cowboys and their lead singer was our lead guitar player and we shared a drummer. We'd go play whatever random gigs we could put together," Neil said. Todd and Neil shared a two-room apartment in an alleyway. Neil also taught guitar lessons to a daughter of the owner of the barbecue trailers, so there was always a brisket in their refrigerator.

Chris was a neighbor and a music student. Neil knew he was very accomplished on the guitar. It was during this time that the Impotent Horny Toads disbanded. "The sound that we were putting out with the Impotent Horny Toads wasn't really what I heard in my head and I couldn't get it across how to fix it. Todd and I were playing our duo shows. Todd was my neighbor during those days and he broke his leg at a wedding in Marathon. So, he bought a harmonica and a Mel Bay 'How to Play Harmonica' book. I hear the vaguest resemblance to 'When the Saints Go Marching In' coming over the cinder-block fence," Neil said. So he decided to go over and jam with Todd. Neil asked whether Todd was tired of playing that song and told him the key was C. Todd knew some songs in that key and they started playing. "I think it took two open mike nights in Terlingua to get Todd to come out of his shell and start playing. You look back at all of us from when we were twenty-three; Todd might have even been twenty. I don't know if he was old enough to drink yet," Neil said.

Chris McWilliams lived upstairs and would come by every day with his guitar. Neil and Todd would ask him to come play with them. When he agreed to jam one afternoon, it was short-lived. "He sits down and opens his case. He took thirty seconds of a listen, shut his case and said, 'No. I can't do this country music.' In his defense, we probably weren't that good at playing country music either at that point. He could probably play from Chopin all the way to AC/DC. He hadn't found the vibe in country music that we discovered that reeled him into it," Neil said. Chris later told Neil that what changed his opinion was hearing Neil play one of his original songs.

Chris went on to finish his degree in music at Sul Ross. Neil saw him play the baby grand piano in a recital onstage there. Neil's main instrument is the bass guitar. He also sings and can "noodle and strum" on the acoustic guitar. "I can do just enough to embarrass myself on a mandolin. About the same on a harmonica. If I would get off my hiney and get a trombone or tenor saxophone, I played those in junior high band so I know I could bring that back

a little bit," he said. Neil also performs solo and currently has a regular gig called Turquoise Tuesdays performing at Eve's Garden, an environmental bed-and-breakfast in Marathon.

Neil owns a fence contracting business and also seals water tanks and builds roads with his crew. "Right now, I've been on a ranch south of Marfa for the better part of three years and I may be there for another decade. They've bought some more property so we're building roads and putting in gates—you know: anything a moderately smart redneck who paid attention in geometry and calculus can do. If I can do the math on it, I can build it," he said.

Todd Elrod grew up in New Braunfels, Texas, home of the legendary music venue Gruene Hall. He came to the Big Bend to attend Sul Ross State University and earned a degree in general studies. Sul Ross offered basic blacksmithing classes, and it was there Todd found what he wanted to do in addition to music. "They offered blacksmithing one and two, part of their farrier program that they had for a good many years," he said. His roommate suggested he take the course. "I fell in love with it from the first time that forge fired up and I got to heat some iron," Todd said. He now owns Broken Anvil Blacksmithing and does custom ironwork. "I get everything and anything, from custom copper bracelets to curtain rods to handmade gates, whatever anybody is willing to pay for. My work is finally getting up to the quality where they're liking it and discovering it, so they're providing me with work and letting me do what I want," he said. His business has been expanding, not only with the part-time residents of the Big Bend, but with the locals as well. His original designs can be seen throughout the Big Bend on ornamental gates and other projects.

Todd arrived in Alpine in 2001 and began working for musician Yadon Hardaway, a member of the Spur of the Moment band, as their roadie. He had grown up around music, since his family lived only three miles from Gruene Hall. "As a kid, I'd just go to Gruene Hall and shoot pool and ride my bike around and hang out.

Chris McWilliams.

Just being in the oldest dance hall in Texas, that was always something I wanted to do, but in high school, I was always playing sports and just couldn't focus on music. When I came out here to Sul Ross, me and a young friend of mine went and crashed a wedding in Marathon; we were young and macho. He knew the band, and we got to wrestling, and a little light rain came down and he came and tackled me and broke my leg. So, I had a few months of spare time," Todd said. During his forced inactivity, he read a book on how to play the harmonica and would sit outside and practice. When Neil joined him on the guitar, they played everything they knew in C, and then Neil suggested that Todd needed more than one harmonica. Todd explains the different harmonicas: "There's diatonic and there's chromatic harmonicas. So a chromatic harmonica has all the keys and you've got a button. You push the button and it switches it a half a note and so you've got all the keys. Whereas diatonic, there is A through G or flats or sharps and they make them individually, so each diatonic harmonica has ten holes. And each one is if you draw or suck, you get a different note."

Todd brings out the cases with his harmonicas, an impressive display. Each harmonica is individually suited to the music being played. "Most songs are in a certain key so I just pick up the one harmonica unless we switch. A song is usually set up of three keys. If you're playing in C, you play C, G, and D, so I just pick up the C harmonica and play with that, and each song has a different note," he said. "I wanted to play harmonica. I always wanted to play music and then when I broke my leg, I had enough time. Everybody else was playing guitar, so I didn't want to do that; I picked up the harmonica instead. That's the beautiful thing about harmonica. As long as you're in the right key you can't sound too bad," Todd laughed.

He plays old blues standards by ear, applying his own style to what is being played. He also has been working on playing the mandolin, fiddle, and a vibraphone, which he describes as a xylophone with a motor

on it. "It's used for jazz. That was my grandmother's and when she passed away my sister got it, and since she isn't the musician of the family she gave it to me," Todd said.

When Neil, Todd, and Chris were students, they would participate in open mike night at La Kiva in Terlingua on Wednesdays and were able to perform with the local musicians at the time such as Pablo Menudo and the regulars on the Porch. "There's a lot more people that are coming in that are wanting to play music and going there just for the little music scene in Terlingua and in the area. Things are growing. There are more musicians out here now. We've got some young people coming out here from Austin and other places. They're checking it out. They're tired of it over there and they like to come over here and play," he said. Todd has also performed in Austin with Mike and the Moonpies, who call him up to the stage to play. When Brian Bingham was performing in Austin, he heard Todd play his regular Friday night gig at the Holland Hotel and later that evening called Todd onstage to play with his band.

As most musicians learn, it can be difficult to make a paying gig worthwhile. Since the distances are considerable in the Big Bend, time and travel expense are serious considerations. For one gig, Neil, Todd, and Chris were paid $600 for the three of them, but since it ended up being over twelve hours, it wasn't even minimum wage. "You go down there, you wait and you're just sitting around waiting hours to play. You set up, get ready in thirty minutes, and then four hours later we play for two hours and leave," he said. "We have fun and when we do get money it's a real bonus and a real treat, but I play for free with all sorts of folks. I do enjoy getting to make a little money on the side too. That helps."

Todd also writes a lot of poetry, which could be set to music. His recording of his original song "Chicago" can be heard on YouTube. Todd's musical style was influenced by the German music of Central Texas. A harmonica, played a certain way, can sound like an

Todd Elrod.

accordion, which Todd does on certain songs, particularly since norteño music, popular in the area, always uses the accordion.

Christopher McWilliams is the other member of the Doodlin' Hogwallops. He was born in Austin but grew up in San Antonio from the age of two, when his US Air Force father was transferred there. Chris came to Alpine to enroll at Sul Ross. His best friend had moved to Alpine first, and when Chris decided to leave San Antonio he came to Alpine and embraced the Big Bend life. Since he was enrolling in college, his parents were appeased. Once Chris moved to Alpine, he never left.

His early influences in music included his mother, who played the piano, and an uncle who studied to be a concert pianist in college. "I was just surrounded by pianos and I always gravitated towards them. I always loved music. Hard to know exactly when I started with it. My dad liked rock and roll so I got a record player when I was very young. I loved rifling through records," Chris said. "I was in orchestra in middle school and I played the violin, the cello, and the double bass. I used to have to carry that double bass home. They wouldn't let me on the bus and I was three-foot-nothing tall at the time and I was lugging that a mile and a half home while the bus would drive by and the kids all laughed at me."

Chris met Neil through a mutual friend on his first trip to Alpine. Chris and his friend had been on a hike up the mountain in the middle of the night. "We came back down the mountain and we were going up to the dorm and I see this guy around the corner, in a leather jacket. He looked like Elvis and he was smoking a cigarette. He was the very first person that I met in Alpine," he said. After they all moved out of the dorms, they were living across the street from one another and began spending time together. "Neil started picking up the guitar and trying to learn stuff. Todd and Neil were trying to play together and I was in the music program, so I had guitars and trumpets. I was already recording albums and writing my own music. They wanted me to play with them and I expressed my disinterest in doing so because they weren't very good. Todd loves to tell the story about how I was too good to have anything to do with them. But then we became friends. I was in another group. I was playing bass, gigging, doing the school thing, and playing shows with that, but I wanted to get out into the music scene and play original music," Chris said.

Chris is a prolific songwriter and enjoys playing Neil's music in addition to his own. "I've always been creative. It's just kind of my nature. It's an extension of having something to do with your hands, or something pleasing to look at, or to hear. I've always been fascinated with words and rhyme. The people who do that kind of thing, I'm fascinated with them. I always thought those people were just the most interesting people on earth. They're creators. I've always endeavored to be that, whatever it was, for better or worse," he said. Chris has been recording music since he was thirteen. He has written a symphony, writes chamber music and string quartets, and wrote a concert band piece that was performed while he was in college. "I got a great music education at Sul Ross and I didn't want to leave. I just wanted to keep going to class and auditing, but you get to a point where you have to go. I tried to get into a bigger music school but I didn't want to leave the Big Bend either, because it's just part of my soul now," he said.

He loves playing honky-tonk music with the Hogwallops for the band setting, and he performs solo

and composes music for ensembles. In the beginning, Chris was not a fan of country or honky-tonk music. "When I was a kid I used to hate country music. I was into music, but I just couldn't get into country. I just didn't want to ever dress like them. I didn't want to wear a dang cowboy hat, and I knew I would have to wear jeans and go to the rodeo. My mother forced me to at times and it was just torture. So, I kind of associated everything about country music with that. Now all I wear is jeans. My parents are divorced, so I always kind of gravitated toward my dad. He liked rock and roll," Chris remembers.

What changed his mind, besides Neil, was working in a feedstore in San Antonio and meeting cowboys and ranchers. He heard a Don Williams song and was intrigued by the lyrics. He began playing the acoustic guitar, which is a standard instrument in country music. His musical tastes are very eclectic and range among classical, blues, jazz, rock and roll, and country.

The change Chris sees in the music scene in the Big Bend has been in the locations of the gigs they play. "The places that people like to enjoy music have typically been bars or parties—outdoor desert parties or something of that nature. We get most of our bread and butter from playing weddings. It's certainly not a really creative environment, but it will give you enough funds in order to play, because we don't make a lot of money playing the bars. The real fun gigs where people are actually into the music are usually not well-paying gigs even if they pay at all," Chris said.

He does not see an aging-out process in their audiences. The older people still come, and the younger crowds come in later. "I think what we do is sort of ageless in that respect. No matter what age you are, you like good music. Some of the specific places are more geared to dancing and some are more geared to drinking. We kind of fill both requirements. Some other places are more quiet and we fill that requirement with the more low-key, acoustic setting. So we've kind of molded our approach to what the crowds were," Chris said.

Typical of the Big Bend, where bands are very versatile, the Hogwallops can deliver whatever music is needed for a gig: four hours of rock and roll, honky-tonk dance, ballads, or old songs. "The music business is a hard business to begin with, but we're in an isolated area and so what you have is a syndrome where you have your hard-core fans who come out to see you a dozen times a year. But every time we play there's always going to be someone who has never heard it, and there is always going to be somebody who has. We have a harder time reaching a big audience," he said. "We play on the radio constantly either in Marfa or here and I guess it reaches the area, but even then, people don't consume music that way here. They consume it more in a live setting. There is a vibrant scene. It's just hard to see because it's so spread out."

The Swifts

Chris Ruggia, Amelie Urbanczyk, Tony Curry, and Eden Hinshaw are the members of the popular band the Swifts, based in Alpine. Tony, Eden, and Amelie were at the interview, and Chris participated by phone at Eden's Pretty Bird Salon.

"I've been in Alpine since the end of 1994 and before that I was in Austin going to college where I met my wife, Ellen. So, we moved to Alpine so she could go to Sul Ross and then I met Amelie a couple of months later when she moved to Alpine," Chris said.

Tony Curry is the youngest member of the group. He has been coming to the Big Bend since he was a child. "My grandfather used to bring us out here with the river rats. Then my dad moved here in 1990 to go to Sul Ross State University and work on his geology degree. I love it here and wanted to stay. So, I found a career as a plumber," he said.

Amelie also became familiar with the area as a child. "My parents brought us to Big Bend a lot, the national park, as children, my siblings and me. When they decided to retire here they asked if I would come to Alpine to help them sort of fix up the house that

they bought that had been rented out to college students and was a big mess. So I moved here just for three months to help them fix up their house and that was in 1995," she said.

Eden has known Amelie thirty-one years since their college days at the University of North Texas in Denton. She met Chris in 1996. The second move to Alpine was the permanent one for Eden. "I came out first because of Amelie. I moved out here in '97. I'm from Austin and I followed her and I was single and career-less and I loved it here. But it was not the time for me, and I thought that I would like to come back someday. So, I went back to Austin, got married, became a hairdresser, and since Austin has grown exponentially, we decided to move here," Eden said.

Tony has a striking speaking voice and is now developing his singing. He credits the other Swifts for helping him to find that voice. He also plays the *cajón*, an instrument originally from Peru. It is a box drum that is played by brushing the front or back with brushes, sticks, or hands and fingers. "Eden loves it when Tony sings because she gets to play the cajón, which is Tony's instrument, but he can't play and sing yet," Amelie said. Tony adds that you sit on the cajón and play, and it has a nice bass sound.

Amelie plays the guitar, the ukulele, and the egg in addition to harmonizing and singing. "The little egg is a percussive instrument that you shake," said Eden. "It's like one of those plastic Easter eggs with tiny beans inside," said Amelie. Chris adds, "It's like a maraca without a handle." The Swifts are the only band in the area who incorporate Peruvian instruments into their music.

Eden and Amelie continued to play music together after college, when they met Chris and began playing with him. When Eden moved to Alpine for the first time, she played with him, and when she moved back the second time, they decided to perform seriously, adding Tony to the group. "We played at music nights where there's a monthly music festival or monthly music jam where you sit around a fire. Musicians

The Swifts. *Left to right*: Tony Curry, Amelie Urbanczyk, Chris Ruggia, and Eden Hinshaw.

under the stars in a circle," said Tony. "There's a guy with a sitar in town, there's a bunch of horns in town. You get some really obscure instrument out of the woodwork, and man, we're just going around the circle, jammin' out to some Foghat or something."

Eden and Amelie note that it is unusual for a band to have two women, making up fifty percent of a group in an area that was dominated by males for so long. They credit the female musicians of the 1970s through the 1990s, particularly the JUGS, with blazing the trail.

Eden explains how the environment affects their music "We choose things kind of diplomatically. We bring songs that we like to the table and then we decide whether or not they're appropriate for us. Also Chris and Ellen write original songs. We choose things that reference Mexico. We choose things that have a lot of distance in them, traveler yearning or openness. When I think about how the people in the audience respond, that's part of how this area has affected our choices and affects how people respond to our music. It's a feeling and therefore, it crosses all types of genres."

The Swifts perform a wide range of genres. Eden likes songs that are bluesy, such as a song Chris and Ellen wrote about New Orleans. Eden calls it a bluesy vignette. They also play some songs that are more country-western. She enjoys playing the Elvis Costello song "Blame It on Cain," which brings their audience out onto the dance floor.

When asked to describe their sound, Chris said, "We have a really intimate sound. We can't play loud because we do a single mike and it feeds back if we turn it up too much. We try to have a real mix of energies. What's an upbeat song for us might be a midtempo for somebody else. It's a pretty low-key sound that we have. The engagement that we get from the crowd tends to be one-on-one: really a strong emotional engagement with a small group. We can't predict what song that's going to happen with on an individual show or any given show."

Each member of the band brings his or her own musical influences to the group. Chris cites Eden's love of Americana and Rodney Crowell, a singer-songwriter of country music and old-school country. Amelie and Eden also bring the influence of the Gourds from Austin, an alternative country and blues band. "Amelie loves the Who. She's the only one in the band who really, really loves the Who," said Chris. He brings songs from R&B, funk, soul, hip-hop, and punk. One of his favorite songs to play is "Keys to Your Heart" by the 101ers, the band that preceded the Clash.

Tony offers a completely different influence to the Swifts. "Keeping up with my kids, I listen to a lot of modern alternative rock and hip-hop. It can be exhausting sometimes, but I like to bring some of the stuff from modern alternative rock to the table. My alternative rock was Nirvana and now the new one is Alt-J, but some of these newer songs that they're coming out with, they're fun to slow down and turn into a bluesy-sounding song and just kind of change up the way that it sounds. It's fun putting a spin on it," he said. Eden remarks that they do a hybrid of Lou Rawls and Sam Cooke. The group brings together all these different sounds and establishes the continuity through the guitars and harmonies. They do perform a few Mexican songs and also note that they play a lot of songs about towns and cities, such as "Tampa to Tulsa," "Detroit to Buffalo," and "Biloxi."

The Swifts perform a few times a month in most of the musical venues of the Big Bend including Alpine, Marfa, Marathon, and outside the area in Fort Stockton and Big Spring as well as for events and festivals. They capture a musical style that differs from straight dance band offerings. Their style would be equally at home around a campfire or in an intimate urban nightclub.

The Resonators and Mariachi Santa Cruz

John Ferguson is the mayor of Presidio, an accomplished and successful musician, a counselor at Presidio High School, and a passionate advocate for the binational blended community of Presidio and Ojinaga, Mexico. At one time, the residents on both

sides of the border crossed freely between the two countries, sometimes by rowboat, sometimes on foot when the Rio Grande was low during drought years. "I really, really enjoy being mayor a lot, but I don't have an office in City Hall. I don't have a key to City Hall. You know, I'm not a micromanager. We've got some really great people, all of whom have run a city on a daily basis. The city administrator runs the show and the mayor and the city council do policy and the typical kind of functions that a mayor would. One of the things a few people joke about, they call me the mayor of Ojinaga because I have real warm relations with them," John said.

John accompanied us to Ojinaga on several occasions to interview musicians. Clearly at home on both sides of the border, he was warmly received at City Hall, where the interviews took place. Presidio has a population of 4,100 compared to 28,000 for Ojinaga, but the people of both cities rely on each other. For example, the people of Presidio formerly crossed the border routinely for medical care, avoiding the need to travel to Alpine, the nearest hospital on the US side of the border.

"I got a phone call about three weeks ago," John said, "and it was the mayor of Ojinaga and he says, 'Hey, we got a pretty serious fire that's going at the landfill and we can't handle it.' We already had an agreement in place to where we could help each other out. Our fire department rolls across and it turns out those guys were fighting this tire fire with black smoke, and they didn't have any kind of masks."

John's mother influenced him to play an instrument at the age of eight, when he was old enough to join the school band. "We were living in Houston at the time. She said she heard I could be in the band at my school. I said okay. I was a third grader; I just wanted to go outside and play. One day, this big case arrives. It was like a suitcase, and we opened it up, and there was this cornet inside there. It wasn't a new cornet; it was a hand-me-down from my uncle. She said, 'Here's what you're going to play in the band.' So I pop in the mouthpiece and just blow on it. 'How do you make a sound?' She said, 'I think you're supposed to buzz your lips.'" John demonstrates. "'Oh, yeah! You're right, Mom!' So, that was 1972, and I did play in the band for that semester, but then at the end of that year, we moved to Garland. She had me play in a band camp one summer, but I really didn't start back until about sixth grade. I found out that I may not be the most popular kid in school, or the best looking, but darn it, I think I might be able to be the best trumpet player at school."

John came to the Big Bend at the age of fourteen on a family vacation in 1977. The following year, his family came back again. "Before we actually got here, I just didn't know what to expect. I heard that West Texas is rocky and dry. I guess I just wasn't real excited before I actually got here. But, once we came and I saw Big Bend National Park and just West Texas in general, I was in love. I came back periodically, and later on when I was in college, I came a couple of times with my dad during Christmas vacation," he said.

John earned his master's degree in 1987 from the University of Northern Iowa and was waiting for his fiancée, Lucy, to finish school. There were no teaching jobs available in Iowa at that time, since the agriculture sector was depressed. John decided to apply for any available teaching jobs across West Texas. "I sent out letters of application starting in El Paso schools going all the way to, I think, Del Rio, and every school district in between. No sooner had I sent out those letters than I got a call from the principal here at Presidio saying, 'Hey, we got your letter here. We've got a job,'" John said.

Lucy visited John for two Christmases before they married. "I flew into Midland-Odessa and I was scared to death, because you come from Iowa, every inch of land is utilized," she said. "There are fields, and green, and grass, and trees, and then you fly into Midland-Odessa and I thought, 'Oh my God. I don't know if I can do that.' It was in the evening, so by the time we got to the turnoff going to Balmorhea, it was starting to get dark so you couldn't really see any of the scenery," Lucy said. "The next morning, I got up and looked out. Hey, there's a mountain right there. All the roads were just gravel except for this main road. It was everything that I've ever known, turned inside out. Everything. The people, the terrain, the attitudes."

Lucy was a stickler for being prompt and on time for everything, but she learned time is more casual in the Big Bend. "I still struggle with this. I am completely anal about time, and getting things done early, and getting on time, and here it's, you know, mañana. 'Yeah, we'll get to it,'" she said. John remembers when they were invited to a sixteenth of September party for Mexican Independence Day. "We ask, 'What time does the party start?' They say, 'Probably about ten,'" he said.

"That was a school night for us," Lucy added. "We were there promptly at ten o'clock and say, 'We've got to go to school tomorrow.' Finally, about midnight the party gets started, and we're thinking, 'We've got to go to school tomorrow.'"

"By about one in the morning we were looking at each other and saying, 'Are you ready to go?'" John said. Everyone told them the party hadn't even started yet. Because of the excessive heat, a lot of the social life in Ojinaga takes place after dark. "I think it's just a different mentality. You kind of work with what you've got. If it's hot, then we just don't do much during the day," said John. The businesses frequently close for two hours in the afternoon and then open again until seven or eight at night.

Lucy grew up on a farm in northeast Iowa. Presidio and the Big Bend is the farthest thing from her experience growing up. "One of the biggest things that I noticed when I came down too, are that people are just so incredibly gracious. They have very little, but they'll invite you in and give you, just about, the shirt off their back, especially in Ojinaga," Lucy said. Since the Ferguson family frequently travels in Mexico, they are usually asked about safety in traveling there, particularly during this time of increased border security and the building of the wall. Lucy insists that the people are completely welcoming and nice.

John and Lucy have a daughter, Molly, and a son, Maxwell. Both were born in Alpine because, as John points out, if you are from Presidio, your children are born in Alpine, which has the closest US hospital. Molly graduated from Sul Ross State University and is a music educator like her parents. Maxwell is graduating from high school and composes electronic music.

Molly plans to return to Presidio to gain experience with her mother in the high school and work with students in Ojinaga. Her husband hails from Veracruz. "I spend a lot of time in Ojinaga and I saw how much lack of resource there is, but yet, with all that lack of resources they produce amazing music. We have so much on the US side and a majority don't really take advantage of that. So, I would love to be in that environment where I can learn how to use what they have, bring in new ideas, and just learn as much as I can. That's kind of my dream: to go deep into Mexico and just help and learn," Molly said.

Molly was the 2017 Tejano Idol Award winner, an honor comparable to the American Idol Award. "I would describe the music from Presidio to be semi diverse, but at the same time it's a lot of norteño music, which is predominant here. I'm not a fan of that kind of music. I used to be, but it got kind of old, I guess you could say. It's still up and running, but little by little, I see things changing, which I feel is good, because I want people to be more exposed to different types of music. They're just so secluded to that one type. I feel like it's going to be here for a while; it's being preserved, I guess. It's still good," Molly said. "I think Tejano seems to be gearing towards Selena, Little Joe Y La Familia, and it's radically different. Another new thing that's coming in is called *sierreño* music, mountain music. What that consists of is the tuba, bajo sexto, sometimes a guitar, and accordion. It's a much different sound." She further defines it as a combination of norteño and banda, a style that younger people listen to, while norteño still has a large older audience.

Tejano was predominant in the 1980s and 1990s and sometimes used electric drums. When their band the Resonators play, the Fergusons have found that if they play too much Tejano, the audience will ask for norteño. When their family group Mariachi Santa Cruz play, however, they get a different response. "Every time we have a mariachi gig playing Selena songs, that's what people want. It's been a long time, but they still celebrate her music," Molly said.

"She was big everywhere, but with her death there just really seemed to be nobody that could carry the torch after that," John added.

The Resonators and Mariachi Santa Cruz are very popular in the Big Bend, and they perform at weddings, quinceañeras, music festivals, and other events. The Resonators were the opening act for Sunny Ozuna and the Sunliners at the Marfa Agave Festival in 2018. They can move seamlessly between Tejano—showcasing Molly's talent—and the more common norteño. Among their favorite songs to play

Molly Ferguson and the Resonators, opening for Sunny Ozuna at the Marfa Agave Festival, 2018.

are "Corrido de los Mendoza," "El Columpio," and "Quinientos Novios." In addition to Mariachi Santa Cruz and the Resonators, Molly has been in several groups in Ojinaga with musicians who attend college in Chihuahua. "I'm working on a project right now which is called Ave Phoenix and it's a rock band group in Ojinaga. When summer's here, we get to play, but then everybody goes back to college, and it doesn't really work out. I'm in several groups at Sul Ross, as well as the wind ensemble," Molly said.

John shares the story that Lucy's father had played steel guitar in a country-western band that took the stage at the Surf Ballroom the night after Buddy Holly, the Big Bopper, and Ritchie Valens performed there and subsequently died in a plane crash. He did not visit them in Presidio before he died. "He's an old farmer. He didn't want to leave the animals, or the garden, or whatever," said John. The Fergusons performed for Lucy's parents in their retirement community and surprised the residents with a mariachi concert, a completely different musical experience, especially for most retirees in Iowa.

John has found that there is a demand for live music in Presidio. "When you consider there's Ojinaga, a city of twenty-five, thirty thousand people over there, and you've got Marfa, which is a destination, people are always needing live music, and we've been playing, in some shape or form, since 2004. We first started with the Resonators, which is kind of a party band. We play for wedding dances, quinceañeras. We're going to play July Fourth in Alpine. We're all pretty strong musicians, but we don't have any illusions about someday maybe

getting famous, because all of us have day jobs. Right now, there's about seven of us," John said.

"It can grow up to nine, depending on who's in town," Lucy added.

"So, you see, we're very blessed in that Lucy and I both play horns, and so our band is a really strong horn band. Horn bands can play some of the Earth, Wind, and Fire songs, just any kind of horn band rock, but then you've got cumbia. You've got Tejano. You've got some of the old music, like jamambo, and cha-cha-cha," John said.

Mariachi Santa Cruz translates to "Holy Cross Mariachi." "Is that religious? No. This little mountain right here is called La Sierrita de la Santa Cruz," John said. There is a mariachi school in Presidio, a growing movement in schools in the Southwest. "When we had a mariachi director here a couple of years ago, every time she went out of town she'd have directors come up to her and say, 'Hey, are you going to move? Are you interested in coming? They're going to make me do a mariachi and I need somebody to come teach,'" Lucy said.

John and Lucy will not leave Presidio; it is their home, where they raised their children and established their careers. "I've always personally considered a promotion as just becoming a better educator, not more money. It would be great to make more money, but that's not what I'm after. I'm not after going to a program where you have to line up six years of straight sweepstakes trophies. We've been here long enough to have seen the results of our work and others, all of us working together. It's pretty gratifying to see these kids be successful," John said.

10

Solos and Duos

LIFE IN THE BIG Bend has created a sort of easy-come, easy-go approach to music making for those who perform here. As already indicated, musical alliances form when people move into the area, then dissolve for a time as others move away. In the same way, musicians may create solo acts or join with another picker for a while. It can be difficult to keep track of who is playing with whom—or who is going it alone—at any given time, but the musicians of the Big Bend aren't too concerned about keeping score.

Yadon Hardaway

Yadon Hardaway lives in Alpine and is a regular performer with the Spur of the Moment band. He was born in Fort Stockton but was raised on a ranch in Marathon. He has known Craig Carter since he was seven years old. His father was a roughneck in the oil fields but moved his family to Marathon, where he became a ranch foreman for twenty-eight years.

He began playing the guitar because of his father's influence. "My daddy played guitar and was a good guitar player and a very good singer but was very shy, and he couldn't play in front of a crowd. We played in church

and he would sit behind the piano and play his guitar so nobody could see him." His father was most comfortable playing with a group of friends. "He could sit in a group of people with his friends, around the living room, and just play and sing and have a big time. But when he got in front of people it was over," Yadon said.

Yadon attended Sul Ross State, moved to Wink, and worked on the Chevron pipeline for ten years. When the oil business crashed he moved back to Alpine with his wife and family. He began performing with the Country Nightriders in 1988, a very popular local band. "We played lots of dances. In the eighties, early nineties, you could play a show at the civic center, have five hundred people in the house. It would be packed. There would be a line of people waiting to come in wanting to go dancing. It's not like that anymore. It's totally changed. Not as many people get out," he said. The musicians talk about the lack of attendance at dances now and conjecture that the tightened DUI laws have changed that, along with the aging out of the population. "Music has changed. People don't dance like they used to. The young people like to stand and watch and go to a concert, where we played mostly dance music."

Yadon Hardaway and his five-string electric bass.

Craig Carter is a prolific songwriter, and the band plays many of his original songs in addition to country music. Yadon explains the hybrid music that is Craig's trademark: "The kind of music that Craig Carter, Ted Arbogast, and Los Pinche Gringos play, it has a little bit different flair. It's Texas music, Texas country, the older Texas country, with the Mexican influence. Most of Craig's songs have that. I kind of consider him the leader and the songwriter on those, on border country," Yadon said.

Besides Craig, Charlie Thomas, Zack Casey, and Yadon are the core of Spur of the Moment. They also play old-style country music that makes people want to dance. "We play a lot of dances. And we like that music. When you play that old music you see people get up and dance. When you kick off with 'Fraulein' or 'There Stands the Glass,' some of those old Ray Price songs, a lot of the old Ray Price swing music, people get up and dance. We're a dance band; if people aren't dancing we kind of feel bad. So the core of Craig's band, we go back to that. We try to bring that into everything. I know we do. It's just in us. We have fit it to Craig's music and his is a little different," he said. The more contemporary country music they play is some Alan Jackson, George Strait, and Willie Nelson.

Yadon grew up listening to the Grand Ole Opry and his father's eight-track tapes in his old Ford pickup. They listened to Ray Price and Merle Haggard. If the weather was clear, they could pick up radio stations.

He performs with Craig Carter seven to ten times a year. Craig spends time away on movie sets but flies back if the gig pays well enough. "Craig's are the ones where we travel a long ways. We've got a gig that we play every year in California. We leave here and drive seventeen hours to go play that gig," Yadon said.

Yadon, Charlie, and Zack have a trio they call the Honky Tonkers. "We play the old dance music, and Zack's an old rock and roller so he throws in some pretty good rock and roll songs. We've been play-ing every weekend. We played the last five gigs in

Fort Stockton. We play a lot of ranch parties. So we've been playing a lot. Every time we turn around we book something somewhere."

The Honky Tonkers are not concerned with the amount of money they can make from a gig. Their performances are usually close to home, and they play a lot of parties. They perform mainly for the love of playing their music. "Zack and Charlie and I love to play music. It's not about the money at all because there is no money in what we do. If it pays for fuel and gets me there and back, we just love to play, so we play a lot. We drive. Most of the gigs aren't far; most of them around here are pretty close," Yadon said.

He has made his living in Alpine, first with his own construction company, now with his spray foam insulation company, but his heart is in the music.

The Border Blasters

Jimmy Ray Harrell and Todd Jagger are the Border Blasters, a popular band that began in Austin, performing under the name Too Much. They played at such well-known venues as Armadillo World Headquarters, the Broken Spoke, the Saxon Pub, and the Split Rail. Todd plays the mandolin and guitar and sings. Jimmy Ray plays the piano, accordion, and guitar and also sings. Todd moved to Fort Davis in the Big Bend in 1991; Jimmy Ray came in 1992. They describe their music as "cowboy swing and hillbilly blues."

Jimmy Ray is from Austin. "I'm a sixth generation Austinite. My family's land was given to make Austin in 1837. They came to Texas in 1833. I came out here to get away from all that, because Austin's way too big," Jimmy Ray said. When Todd called him and said there was a house for rent in Fort Davis for $225 a month, Jimmy Ray said he would be there the next day. That was twenty-six years ago, and he is still there.

Todd was drawn to Fort Davis because it is a good place to raise a family. Both men still have ties to Austin, since Todd's daughter lives there and although Jimmy Ray's large family has mostly dispersed, he still

has family there. "My family is all real spread out, and the Harrells in Austin are not what they were when I grew up. I'm the last of five boys, so we all had our family ties there but everybody's gone in different directions. There's still cousins, and anybody that's got a name even close to mine, we're probably kin," he said.

Todd and Jimmy Ray began playing together in 1975. "I had played in another group before that and Todd was just barely getting out of high school. He and a couple of his other buddies used to come and jam with my partner and me at the time. My partner and I split up; she wanted a band and I didn't. She ended up taking off to go play with a band. Our first gig was at Gruene Hall on New Year's Eve 1975," Jimmy Ray said.

Once they were living in Fort Davis, Todd told Jimmy Ray it was better being a little fish in a big pond than a big fish in no pond. Jimmy Ray has been a builder and currently paints houses. Todd worked for his father's real estate company and started an internet company in Fort Davis.

Todd remembers when he met Jimmy Ray: "The Saxon Pub, that's where I met them. He had the gig at Saxon Pub with his other partner. My friends went down. It was when it was still on the I-35 frontage road in Austin. Went down there and sat there and listened and I don't even think I knew how to play the mandolin at the time. I maybe knew a little bit, but I remember getting up there and acting like I was doing something," Todd said. When they first started playing, they called themselves Duval's Step; Jimmy Ray lived off Duval Road, and "Step" indicated that their music was always danceable.

While performing as Too Much, they released a cassette of their recordings. "Back in the mid- to late eighties, the goal was to get a record deal. There was no infrastructure like there is now for the music business. You needed somebody to bankroll it because making a record was expensive," Todd said. "You could go record it on your own and shop it as a demo, but actually getting it pressed and released cost tens of thousands of dollars." Rob Klein at Waterloo Records introduced

The Border Blasters: Todd Jagger (*left*) and Jimmy Ray Harrell.

them to Alvin Crow's drummer, T. J. "Tiny" McFarland, whom Todd describes as a giant in the Austin music scene. He was a promoter. They recorded at Lone Star Studios with engineer Joe Gracie, who coproduced with Jimmy Ray and Todd. With musicians such as Alvin Crow, Danny Levin, and singer-songwriter Kimmie Rhodes on vocals, the recordings did well on independent radio stations. "We laid it down in two days," said Todd. "We recorded originally twenty-four songs in about twenty-four hours," added Jimmy Ray. They were in the top ten of independent radio stations in Dallas.

Todd was playing with the Austin Lounge Lizards, and Jimmy Ray was also playing with other groups in addition to performing with Too Much when Todd decided to move to Fort Davis. The cassette tape was stored for the future in an army rocket box. "Thank goodness they were in a rocket box!" Todd said. "About 2007, digital was just coming on and I thought we needed to digitize these two-inch master tapes for posterity. So I called a friend of mine who worked as a hotshot engineer in Nashville and said, 'Hey, we have these two-inch master tapes. Is there some way to get that digitized?' He said, 'That's an everyday occurrence here, but try in Austin.'" No one in Austin was able to do that, so he sent the tapes to Nashville to Independent Mastering.

The process involved baking the tape in a one-hundred-degree oven. "Nobody in Austin had the machine anymore to do it. So I sent them off to Nashville and he had to bake them. That's what they have to do. It's a one-time thing; either it works or it doesn't," Todd said.

"The tape literally disintegrates as it goes through the head, so if you don't get it, it's gone," said Jimmy Ray. The process worked and when Dave Sinko heard it, he realized there was some remarkable music there and suggested they release it. He mixed it and included parts that were alternate takes as well.

"So that was what was released as *Blast from the Past*, because it was basically twenty years after the fact," said Todd.

Todd Jagger.

When it was released it made the Freeform American Roots chart as the number 3 CD of 2008. "It got a lot of airplay in Europe. We still get airplay in Europe and here as well. Now, with Spotify, everything is in the cloud, all digital, so we get our fourteen cents every six months on royalties," said Jimmy Ray. They have also released a CD with Sun Records.

The band's current name, Border Blasters, was inspired in some ways by the radio stations of the 1940s and 1950s along the border. "They would play hillbilly, blues, cumbia, and it was all on one thing. So that's kind of where our musical roots are—from Bob Wills to Freddy King to Floyd Cramer to Willie Nelson to Greezy Wheels," Todd said.

Jimmy Ray Harrell.

The Border Blasters still perform in the Big Bend, but the venues have changed. "That thrill part's gone, you know, playing a bar. We might play a private party or a house party, or a public event," said Jimmy Ray, "a nonprofit event or something like that." "Playing bar gigs is fun sometimes, but the driving home late is not such fun," added Todd.

Grupo de la Paz

Ricardo "Rick" Ruiz and Tony Lujan started performing in Alpine at Our Lady of Peace Catholic Church in 1994. They were part of a mariachi group called Mariachi de la Paz. They found talented musicians in the Spanish choir and began performing.

Tony Lujan was born and raised in Alpine. "I've been away a few times because I used to travel. The music was my profession for a while so I've traveled quite a bit. Came back, based out of here, and then was gone again, back and forth. Finally, when my kids were growing up I decided to settle down and stay here," Tony said. He is a longtime employee of Sul Ross State University in the General Services Department. "It's been a long, long, good forty-two, forty-three years of my life that I've spent in the music business. Since I was in high school, actually," he said. His high school band was called the Moonlighter Band. They played a variety of music to reflect their location near the border, but Tony feels his roots are in rock and roll. Since the Alpine radio station did not play rock and roll at that time, Tony found a way to hear it. "I used to sit at home in the evenings. I had a little transistor radio and I could get Oklahoma City, so that's where I would listen to the music I like. Of course, back then the British invasion had just come in and so that's a lot of my roots actually," he said.

Rick Ruiz was born and raised in El Paso, graduated from Eastwood High School in 1984, and then went into the Catholic seminary. "I was in music ministry, youth ministry and that kind of pulled me into the ministry and that ball just kept rolling. So I was ordained a priest and rolled on to music more and more." Rick was assigned to the large parish of Saint Pius in El Paso but was transferred to Our Lady of Peace in Alpine in 1994. He left the priesthood in 2004. "Our music was really not that danceable. Sometimes when our trumpet player and our bass *guitarrón* left, there goes our mariachi idea, so we kind of morphed into Grupo de la Paz, which is more international, more fluid," he said. Their first gig was at Railroad Blues in 1994.

Rick was already familiar with the Big Bend before he was transferred to Alpine. "I did an internship in Marfa back in the late eighties. That's when I fell in

Grupo de la Paz: Tony Lujan (*left*) and Ricardo "Rick" Ruiz.

love with this area. We would do different missions and things. As seminarians, we did a mission when the tornado hit in Saragosa in 1985 or '86. That was a huge impact on me as far as getting the flavor of the people here, the lifestyle, and the closeness of the community. When I was assigned to Alpine it was a fit for me. It was a wonderful time as a priest. No regrets . . . no huge regrets, anyway. After a while, my focus was more on music and it continued that way," he said.

"I'm very thankful for that, believe me," Tony adds. "I don't know who sent him over here, but I give thanks for that person because this guy, we've just become so close, you know, like brothers and family."

Tony raised his family in Alpine and is a grandfather now. He believes Alpine was a good place to raise children. Rick has a daughter in Midland.

Rick and Tony stay as busy as they want with music gigs. "We are blessed to be in a huge tourist economy. We're blessed to have Sul Ross State University. We're blessed to have a population that celebrates everything. That keeps me busy. I also play at services, at funerals, weddings, ceremony services. So we do a little bit and then on weekends, click it up a notch usually. The Gage Hotel has been wonderful. I have regular weekly gigs, which, even for people in Austin, is unheard of," Rick said. "They have to pay the owner of the bar to play [in Austin]. There the cost of living, because of the tech industry and everything, rent is high. We do weddings sometimes once, twice, three times a month and even musician friends in El Paso say 'wow, we're lucky to even have one wedding,' which is big as far as our bread and butter goes.

We don't all get to play all the time, but I have something to sustain my income."

Rick and Tony play the guitar and Rick does most of the singing. Grupo de la Paz has had up to seven people performing, depending on the gig, sometimes adding violins, flute, sax, and trumpet players. "The core is myself, Tony on guitar, Jimmy is our drummer. He's actually my nephew. The three of us are A Few Too Many," said Rick. They play a variety of music, including country, rock, and a lot of Spanish music. "Boleros, cumbias, corridos, waltz, and a lot of times those come together beautifully. Waltzes in English are the same as waltzes in Spanish. Well, not the same, but they can carry on. We will start one waltz in English and end it in Spanish and everyone seems to like it. I think the music really hasn't changed much because our audience comes from people that have destination weddings in Marathon and they're many times surprised that we can play some R&B. Then we play down-home Johnny Cash and Marty Robbins. We really have to do a variety and we've always done that, I think. Even though we started as mariachi," Rick said. "It depends on the venue too. Some people prefer country, for instance, so we've got a good two sets for country."

"We could actually do a country gig as well as a rock and roll gig. Throw some blues in there, some cumbias. People love that, they love the variety, the versatility that we have," said Tony.

Rick and Tony do not perform original music and do not write their own songs because they enjoy the enthusiasm of the audience when they perform music that has associations with that age group. Rick refers to the baby boomers as their bread and butter.

Tony and his friend Jay Davidson started a band from Presidio, the Resonators, in 2004, and he performed in the group Mariachi Santa Cruz. "We got to be like a nine-piece group with the Resonators and after a while people were starting to complain because there wasn't enough money to support a group that big. We weren't making it; all of a sudden we weren't

making that much money, and the group was growing and it wasn't working out," Tony said.

Tony played country music a lot earlier in his career, traveling with country bands as a singer. He performed with Willie Nelson when he was filming in South Texas. He and Rick are well versed in the large variety of music in the Big Bend.

The Winehouse Amys

Jeff Cowell, older brother of Shanna Cowell of the JUGS, and his brother Stephen are both musicians but do not perform together. Jeff was a drummer and played with numerous bands until he became the lead singer of the Austin band the Rock Busters from 1990 to 1994. He moved back to Alpine in 1995 and changed to playing the ukulele and singing.

Jeff and Steve Martinez began playing together in 1999, and when Jeff returned from Hawaii he told Steve on a trip to Chinati Hot Springs about an instrument he had seen there. "We had gone there for some kind of work weekend and we were helping build some stuff but there was a tub that we were messing around with," Steve said.

"It's a jerry can," Jeff adds.

"I call this the one-string, heavy metal, jerry-can, sotol, fart-box bass, because it's a ridiculous instrument, but it's been fun," said Steve. The instrument resembles a washtub, with an upright stem and neck with a resonating string, but instead of a washtub, the base is a large, army-green, hollow metal container.

Their first gig was Temper Brown's funeral at Brown Ranch on Halloween 1999. "Later that year we went to New York City and played. We were there for Y2K, New Year's Day 2000," Jeff said. Then Steve moved to San Antonio, and they did not perform together until he came back at the end of 2004. They landed a weekly residency at Edelweiss Brewery at the Holland Hotel and played every Saturday for years. They also had an eight-week residency in Marfa at the Saint George Hotel a few years ago. "We have a

The Winehouse Amys: Jeff Cowell and Steve Martinez.

lot of fun in Marfa. We really like the Marfa crowd. We played the Lost Horse and Convenience West," said Jeff. "Marfa has been a very good audience for us. We've appeared on David Branch's radio show and he's a great guy. He's not really a musician or anything, but he's keeping it real out here. He's been an inspiration to me, and to me it's all about searching for inspiration. Once I get inspired, then we're all having a good time."

Their style differs from that of other musicians in the Big Bend, not only in the type of music they play, but in how it is played. "We did not plug in, we had no PA, no amplifiers, even in a big room. That's the way our sound works best. We've been forced to perform in clubs where you have to mike things and run in through a PA, but our sound is pretty organic," Jeff said. Steve knows his instrument sounds best without electronics. "This thing sounds best when the sound you hear is coming from there. If you take it and run it through a microphone and some wires and knobs and all that and regurgitate it, it just comes out as electronic gobbledygook. It's a pretty cave-man, kind of post-apocalyptic instrument," he said.

Jeff notes that there are only five strings in their duo and there is no need for a stand-up bass. "I'm not partial to guitars. I tend to think there's too many guitars out there. A hundred years ago, music was all different voices and instruments and it was music. At some point, it just turned into a bunch of guitars and they built an amp and plugged them in and turned them up real loud and that's about all you get. Any band you see now is going to have two or three guitars in it," he said. His ukulele has nylon strings, and the addition of a guitar with metal strings would drown him out.

Jeff began singing and found he liked that better than drumming. "I was a drummer all my life and played drums in bands in Austin. I was mainly concerned with black T-shirts and evil stuff that happened after midnight," he said. "But as I got older and maybe less angry, we had a band and we couldn't get a good singer, and I decided, 'Well, I can sing. Let's just find somebody who is a good drummer and I'll start

Jeff Cowell.

Steve Martinez.

singing,' and since then I've been a singer. The ukulele is more or less just a prop to me. What I like to do is sing." Jeff brings out his ukulele and sings "Hello, Dolly!" The ukulele seems to fit the song.

He and Steve play classic country with some jazz and rockabilly, but they are unique in performing what could be called bubblegum music and early television theme songs. "We got a good response to our version of the *Flintstones* theme song, the Oscar Mayer jingle, and 'Sesame Street.' One of our new songs is the theme from *Happy Days*, which is a great short song and the crowds respond well to that. Then some Tommy Roe. We play 'Dizzy' and 'Wendy' by the Association. That theme song from *Billy Jack*, 'One Tin Soldier' and the theme song from *The Monkees*. We do 'I'm a Believer,'" Jeff said. They also play some Loretta Lynn, Connie Smith, and Lee Ann Womack. When David Branch played the Amy Winehouse song "Rehab" on his show on Marfa Public Radio, *The Honky-Tonk Happy Hour*, they decided to learn the song and rename the band.

Jeff and Steve have been playing together for over twenty years. Jeff points out that if they had been doing this for the money they would have quit nineteen years ago. Steve works at Big Bend Saddlery and does other leatherwork. Lately he has been making pistol holsters.

Jeff describes himself as an underemployed ukulele player. He has noticed that ukulele music is not popular anymore. "They keep saying it's going to come back and you see them on TV and commercials and hear them in the background of some commercials, but over the last twenty years I haven't seen a great resurgence of interest in the ukulele, and I don't see a lot of artists out there playing it. Even when I went to Hawaii in '97, very few people were playing the ukulele. Mostly it was old people and little kids. None of the tourists seemed to want to hear ukulele," he said.

Steve and Jeff recorded a Christmas album eleven years ago and did a live recording at a Kinky Friedman campaign fund-raiser in Alpine. The number of gigs has decreased, however, as it has for many of the Big Bend musicians and bands.

Matt Skinner

Matt Skinner came from his home in Fort Collins, Colorado, to be interviewed, along with his musical mentor Michael Stevens. Matt began in music in Alpine, where he would hang around in the background with musicians. "I always tell people I was looking for a place to stand that was out of the way. Turned out I was good at it," he said. His family were not musicians, but they liked to dance. "They liked to go to dances, so we started doing that when I was a kid. In the early nineties when I was dragging around an old Japanese guitar, back when Pearl Jam and Guns N' Roses were king, that's what I wanted to be," Matt said.

Michael remembers when he first saw Matt. "I had seen him on the street, this tall, skinny kid with a Japanese guitar, playing with no amplifier, just walking along. At that point, I know he's got the bug. Then he shows up at the show somehow, he probably just heard about it. Everybody comes and bangs on the back door and all kinds of people would show up there," Michael said. Matt's father was the president of the Cowboy Poetry Gathering, and Michael was vice president. Picking sessions developed at Michael's shop, and sometimes as many as fifty people would show up to listen. Matt brought his grandmother's '53 Gibson. That is where he learned to play country songs. "He'd start playing something and we'd just ignore what the hell he played and we played the song, but he could hear it. We just picked him up and went . . . magic carpet! The light came on and that was that. The next time he showed up he had black Ropers, brand-new starched blue jeans, a black hat that looked like he'd borrowed it, and a white shirt," Michael said. That was the customary dress for Michael, Matt's dad, and the other musicians. It was a dramatic departure from Matt's customary cargo shorts and combat boots.

Matt lived in Alpine and went to Brackettville to work as a gunfighter and musician at Happy Shahan's Alamo Village, a tourist attraction. "I put on a cowboy show playing cowboy music for a half-hour show four or five times a day. Then, right after that, there was a gunfight skit right out in the street," he said. After that summer, Matt went to music school at South Plains College in Levelland, where he was able to study with accomplished musicians. Matt and Michael joke about Levelland, where Michael had turned down a job opportunity because it was all plains and no mountains. "In Levelland, if you stare at the horizon, you can see the back of your head," Matt said. "What's that other one that Terry Allen always said? 'It's the only place in the world where you can be up to your ass in mud and have dust blowing in your eyes.' He'd never been to Wyoming, though," Matt adds.

Matt has his own band, the Matt Skinner Band, that regularly performs every Thursday, Friday, and Saturday night. "We play lots of the festivals and some beer joints here and there, and a couple of the bigger theaters. I first started out playing cover songs and then I wanted to be a writer. So the bulk of my set anymore is all original stuff," he said.

His other job is in oil and gas. Typical of the music coming from the Big Bend, his music is cross-genre. He was influenced by the Ojinaga Sound at an early age. "We all grew up going over to Ojinaga and listening to the guitars over there. After church on Sunday, the old man would say, 'Let's go to Ojinaga,' and we'd all pile in the truck and go down and have lunch at Los Comales all afternoon," Matt said. "There was plenty of beer and food and music, and all those bands would just roam through there. Some would be just a solo guitar player and sometimes they'd come through with a full six- or seven-piece band with all the regalia on," he said.

He was interviewed in France once, but they only knew about Nashville. Matt feels he has nothing in common with the music in Nashville, although he spent time there talking to music publishers. Matt did not fit what he calls the "Nashville mold." He likes to be able to recognize the influence of George Jones or Merle Haggard, which is not what the new music

Matt Skinner.

reflects. "Walking into Michael's studio that day with my hat on and my combat boots on, well, that was one of those moments. Take a different turn and that was that moment. So sitting in here listening to these guys for years and years and years, playing, and they were always so patient and gracious. Still are. I was just a sponge," he said.

While performing in the Big Bend, Matt became accustomed to being able to simply call out a song title and the rest of the musicians would join in. That was not the case in Colorado, because there is a strong bluegrass and hard-core honky-tonk bass influence there. Matt thinks that if you know a few Grateful Dead songs, you can get a gig any-where. "People really love that music and anything by Buck Owens. They're really big into rockabilly and truck driver music. It's become its own thing, which comes from country, which comes from rock, which comes from blues, cowboy stuff, you name it," he said. "There's a lot of banjos up there, more banjos in Colorado than I would have thought. Interesting thing about my band, we've got me on guitar. We've got a bass player. We've got a Dobro player and a drummer, if we're playing electric." All the band members play an acoustic instrument. Their drum-mer also plays the mandolin. Matt plays more swing and some blues and finds the style hard to describe. "The community radio station up there, KRFC, has a Tejano segment on it, which I didn't realize they did until driving back in I hit it at just the right moment and it felt like home," Matt said.

Matt's wife was graduating in May 2019 from vet-erinary school in Colorado and they had not decided where to go until she received job offers. She did not have much opportunity to spend time in the Big Bend while she was pursuing her degree. Matt would love to move back to the area. "I thank my dad all the time: 'Thank you so much for not raising me in Dallas.' Nothing against Dallas, but growing up out here was great. You could sort of run wild out here back in the old days. I love it out here," he said.

Gary Oliver.

Gary Oliver

Gary Oliver is an in-demand songwriter and musician and a popular political cartoonist for the *Big Bend Sentinel* in Marfa. He is also legally blind. He signs his cartoons with the name Golliver. He came to live in Marfa in 1982, passing through on his way to Alaska. He had just spent over four years in Central and South America.

Gary grew up in Beaumont. "My folks found out what was going on with my eyes when I was about two years old. I was cross-eyed, the main reason I wear glasses. I have nystagmus. There was nothing they could do for it. When I went to school I used binoculars to see whiteboards; it took me a few grades to figure out I could do that. I used to just have to walk up to put my nose on the board to read what they were writing. I'm also color-blind," he said. He started accordion lessons when he was ten. He was also a cartoonist at an early age. "That's the reason I went to UT. I was winning UIL (University Interscholastic League) cartoon contests in the sixties. That was the only award with the newspaper that my high school got so they had to take me to the convention," Gary said. He likes comic strip art rather than political cartoons, but it is a very tough market. He once drew a comic strip that was published in Buenos Aires.

He came to Marfa because he met a lady who had a house there. For the previous five years he had no longer been traveling most of the year, and he decided to settle down. He began drawing political cartoons for the newspaper and performing music.

Gary's cartoons are popular, but some politically conservative readers have suggested that perhaps he should live elsewhere. His first cartoon for the *Sentinel* was in 1983.

Gary attended the University of Texas at Austin, and when he was a sophomore during the folk era of the 1960s, he learned to play the guitar. Since he knew how to play the concertina, he could play some songs on the accordion. "I'd given up the viola after high

Oliver's biting political satire has raised a few eyebrows in the Big Bend.

Call as well as with other groups. He usually plays the guitar but also plays the accordion and sings or backs up the other musicians. Most of the songs he writes are for guitar.

While living in Austin, Gary and two friends owned a bar they bought from a law student. Gary described his bar as being totally countercultural and himself and his partners as three hippies who couldn't find a job. After running the bar for several years, Gary grew tired of the Austin bar scene and began traveling the world. "I was in the revolution in Nicaragua. I was in a couple of coups. Had to sneak out of Honduras once after a coup by walking over the mountains into Salvador," Gary said. He also lived with a film company in Argentina and lived in Patagonia. He would return to Austin, stay for a month or two, and then travel again. Gary started playing the guitar while he was in Argentina. "I bought one in Argentina literally just so I could learn their songs, because everywhere I went people played guitar. That helped me learn a bunch of Latin American songs. My band has played Paraguayan songs before," he said.

Gary shows us two intricate and beautiful accordions, one a Gabbanelli. He explains the difference between diatonic and chromatic accordions. Norteño music uses the diatonic accordion with buttons, while the chromatic accordion has a keyboard. "Most of the keyboard accordions are chromatic. Doesn't matter which direction the bellows is going. The notes are the same. It's just a way to power a piano, so to speak, with a large set of bass," he said.

The accordion is the staple of norteño music, so there are many opportunities to see it played on both sides of the border. "What always used to amaze me in a café in Ojinaga, we'd go sit down and if you're lucky a little walking band will come in. And if the guy had a trumpet he has to stand across the room because he's so much louder than everybody else, but sometimes those guys walk in with a Gabbanelli. Here's a guy coming in to play you a song for a buck

school. That was too bad, because we need fiddlers out here. There aren't many," Gary said.

Gary believes that performing with a band requires a unique set of abilities. "The skills you need for a band are not the same as the skills you need for sitting around the living room playing a guitar. For instance, last night we had maybe six guitars up there, but a couple of the guys are lead guitar players and that's totally different," he said. "You need a lead and a rhythm. When you play one of these you need a rhythm behind you, but it's great to have a lead so the accordion isn't doing all the melody." He performs with Hall's Last

and he's carrying a five-thousand-dollar piece of equipment," he said.

Gary takes us into his art studio, where floor-to-ceiling bookcases are devoted to cartoonists and their history. It is an amazing collection. "This is basically the history of comics in here. This is Carl Barks's thirty-volume hardback set; he is the guy who created Uncle Scrooge and Gladstone Gander. Not many people get thirty-volume sets of their work," Gary said. His favorite cartoonist is Walt Kelly, the creator of the comic strip *Pogo*.

He drew for Copley News Service for two years, creating cartoons about Mexico, often about Mexican politics. Since Donald Trump was elected president, Gary has found a rich source of cartoon possibilities. "He's the best in a long time for caricature. The best since Clinton. Nobody ever really got a good George W. Bush in the cartoon world. And nobody ever got a good Obama as far as I'm concerned. Trump's hair is just a natural for a cartoon," he laughed.

Ray Freese

Ray Freese lives in Marfa but grew up in Wisconsin, where he met his wife, Christine. They moved from Houston and made Marfa their home twenty years ago. "We heard there was an art community out here and I like open space. I like country. I grew up on a farm. She likes culture so we thought this would be the perfect combination for that. I love the sky, I love the air and the water, I love stars and nature," he said. Now that Marfa is a tourist destination, Ray sees the town as much more active than when he moved there.

Ray was influenced by the music of his foster uncle when he lived on a farm as a child. "I moved there when I was ten years old and I think when I was twelve my foster uncle played in a band, Normydogs and the Melody Boys, a vocal band in Wisconsin," he said. "My life was so stressful, being in children's homes and orphanages until I was ten, that finally getting on the farm and having all this land, since

Ray Freese.

I grew up in the inner city, and playing music was just a release for me."

Ray met Christine in Milwaukee, where he was playing music at a bar called The End of the Line. They immediately connected and knew they would spend their lives together.

In addition to pursuing music, Ray was an audio-visual tech in Chicago and Houston and other big cities. While living in Houston, Ray also worked in guitar shops, drawn to the musicians and the atmosphere.

Ray sings and plays the guitar and piano. He is also a gifted songwriter. He performs his favorite styles of music, which he grew up hearing: R&B or country. He plays with some bands in the area. "Ironically, I played with an Irish band with a tin whistle player and a great violinist. He was from Alpine but moved to Salt Lake City to build violins. That's where they had a dream of making high-end violins. We did all the traditional Irish songs. We would play for ranch parties. At first they were taken aback, but then they realized it wasn't too far off from the two-step music that they were used to," Ray said.

During the interview at his house, Ray's guitar seldom left his hands. He played and sang two of his original songs, including "The Dinosaur Song," a happy and educational song for children that he has performed in schools. Ray also teaches music but does not charge for the lessons. "The reason I don't teach for money is because I don't want that in the way. I really want people to learn and not be restricted by having to pay. That throws me off; it's such an aesthetic thing for me," he said.

Although Ray is retired, Christine is not. She teaches art one semester every year at the University of Kansas in Lawrence.

Ray seldom performs in Marfa except when asked to be part of a group. He does not charge for those gigs, either. A well-known song in Marfa that Ray wrote is "Marfa Dog," which he sings for us. Ray was asked to write this song by a filmmaker who was doing a movie

on dogs living in Marfa. He received a check for $250 for his songwriting. "That was a fun thing to do. When I finally figured out what I was going to do I told my wife and she just laughed about it. It had to do with this dog that would walk back and forth in front of our apartment," Ray said. "We lived where the laundromat is, over the coffee shop that is now in the laundromat. This dog would walk back and forth, day and night, and never pay attention to anybody. Somebody would come around, maybe he would just move over. It was like he had someplace to go."

Ray is a kind and gentle man who is passionate about his music, whether playing or songwriting. In retirement, he is living the life he wants in the place he loves.

Peter Westfall and Steve Sorg

Peter Westfall is a professor of statistics at Texas Tech and planned to retire in May 2019. He is in Alpine nearly every weekend. He performs as Cowboy Pete. He and his wife have a home in Alpine as well as Lubbock. They bought a house in Alpine when their daughter began working at the McDonald Observatory and they came to visit. Although they became deeply attached to the area, it was not economically sensible to rent hotel rooms and apartments, so they bought a home.

Pete got started in music as a teenager. "Like a lot of people, it was just something cool to do, something fun to do. I really loved it a lot. I thought I'd be a musician, so I entered school at the University of California at Davis as a music major. Did fine, but after a year I began to realize that wasn't going to pay the bills. I really wasn't going to be a star, so I decided to become a statistician instead," he said. "I've done that for quite a long time and I've been getting back into music a lot more lately, in the last ten years. This place is a real fruitful area, all these people that are interested in music."

He met Steve Sorg at Harry's Tinaja, where musicians regularly meet and jam. "They've got a guitar there. People just go there and jam, and it's all kinds of people, all kinds of talent. You might have super professional musicians there and just rank amateurs. Kind of what wanders through the area, too," Pete said. Steve played with area bands that originated at Harry's Tinaja. Pete compares it to the Porch in Terlingua.

Pete began on the piano, but his instrument now is the guitar. Although Steve and Pete are both from Northern California, they did not meet until they came to Alpine. Pete grew up listening to the radio stations in San Francisco in the 1960s when Jefferson Airplane, the Grateful Dead, the Jackson Five, and Motown were popular. "I really developed a love for jazz as I kind of got a little more into it. It was just so intriguing. The intricacies of all that. I think I'm sort of more of a harmony person. That's why I need people like Steven to keep me on track because I focus a little bit more on harmonies than on rhythm, but I'm working on that," he said.

Pete performed with his first wife as Bittersweet, playing Carole King and Linda Ronstadt–type songs, and then they had a band called Country Choice. He then pursued an academic career.

Steve and Pete have played in a number of bands. They performed most often with a young singer-songwriter from Abilene named Bland Scott who lived in Valentine. They performed nearly every other weekend at Padre's in Marfa. "Brian Garrison, who no longer lives in Alpine, is extremely talented; he put together the Chuckwagon Show at the Granada. We would go do a dinner theater. There was shtick involved, but there was also good music, and it was for all ages, because he's got a posse of kids. He's got six kids, something like that, and they're all performers," Steve said. Steve and Pete also performed in gigs outside the area in the state.

When they perform, Pete sings mostly harmonies and plays the guitar. Steve sings while he performs as the drummer.

"Here's the hardest part," Steve said. "When you're drumming you're using four limbs. Your voice is like a fifth limb and it's really difficult to coordinate that fifth limb. I can sing harmonies and if the beat that I'm playing is pretty simple, I can do that. But if you try to ask me to sing lyrics while I'm drumming? There are guys that can do it. And a lot of guys, even though they know the song by heart they have the words there. They read the words while they're playing because it enables them to incorporate that fifth limb that they wouldn't otherwise be able to do," said Steve.

They have other musicians performing with them, usually four. At their last gig they played with Gary Oliver and Jim Hall of Hall's Last Call. "Pete can sing half a dozen songs. We didn't have as much time as we have for most gigs so he only went and sang a couple of songs. But it's great because Jim sings a number of songs, Gary sings songs. Pete will also harmonize so it really works out well," said Steve.

Pete Westfall and Steve Sorg.

On Wednesday nights at the American Legion Hall there are informal jam sessions that have become very popular, with up to eight musicians onstage. The players have varying degrees of skill.

Steve moved to Alpine eight years ago when he reconnected with Regina, a former classmate who lived in Alpine, at a high school reunion. Steve's career was in high tech in the Bay Area, and when he turned fifty, he decided to leave. "I came out here and here's the interesting thing: I played in rock bands. I left behind a very good band that's still gigging in the Bay Area. I came out here and I initially got together with a couple of guys to play rock and roll that just weren't going to go anywhere. Did that for a few months," he said. "Then I started playing with Kelly and Allison and Walter Thomas. They were playing a three-piece combo with a drum machine. I introduced myself and told them I could learn these songs and play with them. I didn't know any of the songs because I never listen to country music." Steve impressed them with his playing and he began performing with them. He played blues while in the Bay Area and found that the blues beat transitioned easily into country. "You're doing a lot of shuffles, maybe some train beats and things like that. And that bag of tricks works really well in country music. So, I could apply beats that I knew. I just had to learn the songs," Steve said. Until then, Steve had never listened to country music. "I'd be driving through central California, on my way to backpacking or hunting, and Southern California is just Mexican stations and country stations. I'd just turn the radio off until I'd hit the foothills and I'd get the classic rock or something back on again," he said.

Steve knew from the first grade that he wanted to be a drummer and irritated his teachers by drumming on his desk. He was not allowed to play the drums in the school orchestra until the sixth grade, so Steve played horn in the fifth grade until he could get on the drums the next year.

He was surprised that there were so many gigs in the Big Bend. He substitutes in bands all over the area, such as Los Pinche Gringos and the Doodlin' Hogwallops. Being a drummer means transporting more equipment than those who play simpler instruments. "I have a practice kit at home. It's huge. Drums all around. But when we perform I keep a very simple kit. I have two more kits in addition to that practice kit at home. They're both vintage Ludwig kits from the midsixties. A sparkle which I loved when I was a kid," Steve said.

Steve and Pete play the music popular in the area and see that music as being cross-genre, even in country music. "I guess you can call it the broad classification of country music, out here you have what they call the red dirt music," said Pete.

"It's these younger guys that have been doing original music and it doesn't sound a lot like the traditional country music," added Steve. They name Ryan Bingham and Hayes Carll as examples. "Country, for better or worse, is a lot of just putting new words to tried and true melodies. It's relatively rare when a song comes out that's really original. I like Zac Brown because he's really original. But Brooks and Dunn, their stuff all sounds the same to me," said Steve. "The difference between country music and jazz is with jazz music you've got five thousand chords and five people in the audience. With country you have five chords and five thousand people," Pete said.

Steve and Pete have noticed that their crowds are getting older, and they tailor their performance to what will get people out on the dance floor. "We're driven by what gets people dancing, not so much by what the genre of the song is. Shoot, Jim will pull out 'Old Time Rock and Roll,' the Bob Seger song, and that'll fill up the dance floor," said Pete.

David Beebe

David Beebe came to Marfa from inner city Houston in 2007. He owned and ran live music nightclubs in Houston. He still co-owns one that is a success. "I had an opportunity to build one of those out here. Even though the finances didn't look good for it, I went ahead and took the chance. In retrospect, it was a good thing because I got out here, but I had the wrong business partners, so it failed," he said. The club that he built himself and operated for five years was Padre's. He is relieved not to be doing that anymore.

He is a justice of the peace in Marfa, owns a taco shack, works as a DJ, distributes potato chips, and has worked as a substitute teacher. He is also in two music groups. He plays as a duo with well-known musician Primo Carrasco and also plays bass in a norteño band, Renacer del Norte. "'Renacer' means 'rebirth.' All of us had music careers at one point and now we're coming back. It's true, in a way. It's also kind of funny because none of us really ever hit the bottom," said David. The bandleader is Hector Sanchez; the accordion player is Ismael Medrano, who played with the Ojinaga band Conjunto Amanecer, a famous norteño band who toured for twenty-five years. He moved to Marfa from Mexico to be with his wife. Jesse Rodriguez is the drummer; he and Hector were born and raised in Marfa. "These are good musicians. So, I play in a norteño band playing cumbias and more arranged tunes of those," David says. "Fans say the traditional conjunto bands are a little more jammy. It's been explained to me the difference between conjunto bands from the recent past and norteño bands is with the norteño bands, they are playing conjunto and not just cumbias, they are playing more precise arrangements. There's less of a jammy feel," David said.

When he plays with Primo, it is a very different experience. They play traditional regional Mexican music that David describes as being played very loosely by two people who have learned it by ear. "Primo doesn't know the names of the chords. He never had any formal instruction at all. I had minimal formal instruction, but I have years and years of onstage experience and I've learned a lot as I've gone along," he said.

In the Big Bend, Tejano does not get nearly as much play. David thinks Tejano is not in style anymore. It is more closely identified with the 1980s

and 1990s. "Tejano is more a synthetic sound, it's also lighter. When I was playing in my rock and roll bands in Houston, the most popular local Tejano band was, maybe still is, La Mafia. Excellent band. There's layers of synthesizers, kind of glossy," David said. Tejano is considered lighter than norteño, including the subject matter of the songs. There can still be an accordion in Tejano music, but synthesizers, drums, and horns update it to a different sound. David thinks the end of *puro Tejano* began with the death of Selena.

"Here in this area, nobody gives a doggone about anything except norteño and banda. And banda is that stuff that sounds like a marching band," he said. Banda is very popular in the interior of Mexico and its popularity has expanded to the border. David goes to Ojinaga about once a month to shop and practice his Spanish. He heard the song "Soy Feliz" multiple times while he was there. "It's a banda band and a guy's playing accordion, and he's actually playing piano accordion, which is extremely rare. The whole theory of the song is, 'I'm having a good time. I'm having a great time. When I'm on the beach, I'm happy. When I'm at the house, I'm happy. When I'm just in here, I'm happy. When I'm with the ladies, I'm happy. Woo!' That's the whole song. It's kind of banda, it's kind of norteño. It's kind of a mix. Three months ago, I could go over to Ojinaga and hear it three times a day on the radio," David said. He describes it as a dumb, funny song that you can dance to, since it is a cumbia.

Synthesizers are used in norteño, he says, but the mainstays are the accordion and the saxophone. "I think what people really like is you have an accordion and a saxophone either playing at the same time, playing a line in unison or in harmony, playing a signature line of a song. So, norteño may be a little simpler in a way. There might be simpler chord progressions."

David's norteño band plays George Strait and Freddy Fender songs such as "Before the Next Teardrop Falls," "Wasted Days and Wasted Nights," and "Hey, Baby Que Paso" by Augie Meyers, songs that David believes are the link between rock,

David Beebe.

conjunto, norteño, and country. "'Wasted Days and Wasted Nights' is a soul song. It's a swamp box song. It's a Louisiana swamp box song repurposed as a Monterrey Mexico song as the San Antonio national anthem. It's the same doggone song and it's something for everybody. Primo and I sing it over at Planet Marfa. There's little kids out there dancing around," David said. "There's eighty-year-old men who don't come out of their house except to see me and Primo because we sing 'Las Medias Negras' and 'Cielito Lindo.' We sing these songs that are normally heard only when mariachi bands sing them, but they're the same songs that were popular with your grandparents that you heard growing up that are not forgotten, that are not really recorded that often these days."

David compares the music of Little Joe Y La Familia, with their polished arrangements, to the music of Ojinaga. "Little Joe Y La Familia, they've got a whole lot of accents and they're really like a special brand of conjunto. They're highly arranged. They have a bunch of syncopations that from song to song are similar. The band is very well rehearsed. There's lots of harmonies," he said. "I would say the Ojinaga Sound tends to be a little more stripped down, a little more hard edged. A little more like your recording doesn't have to sound like it cost a million dollars to make to have a hit."

In his band performances, he finds that half the time when they bring in a new song, it will be one that Ramón Ayala covered. They also play country. The song that dancers respond to is "Eu Vou Ver," what David calls the Mexican "Brown Eyed Girl." "It's an anthem. It's a-grown-man-crying music. If people have had a couple of drinks and you want to get them out on the dance floor, you can play anything done by Vicente Fernandez," he said.

David describes Primo's style as operatic. The backup is very simple: David plays the electric guitar and sometimes the *guitarrón*, while Primo plays the guitar. "He plays the guitar and there's no guitar solos. There's no additional instrumentation besides vocals.

There might be a couple of bars where we just break in and play chords," David said.

David is also the secondary vocalist in the bands he plays in and the third vocalist in Renacer del Norte. Most of the gigs with that band are quinceañeras, anniversary parties, and other large gatherings that can last all night. Frequently a DJ will play alternate sets to please the younger people, who prefer rap, while the older people want to hear more traditional music. "The adults want to hear more of the stuff we're playing. The kids also like the cumbias. I think cumbia is the hottest dance in the nation right now, at least anywhere below the Red River. It's by far more popular than rock and roll or country, really," David said.

What surprises David is that more Anglos don't come to the performances of Renacer. When it looked like there would not be a New Year's dance in Marfa one year, David and his band members went to the USO hall and rented it for the night, having to clean it up first, even mop the floor. "I don't remember what we were charging. There was no food provided but we had BYOB and we played all night and there was also a DJ playing between us. We probably had two or three hundred people there, and probably ten or fifteen white folks showed up and stayed for a little while and split," David said. He sees that as a separation, although the music is not segregated to the people who have been listening to it most of their lives. "The separation is not one of bitterness or even anxiety. I think it's just more like a holdover. I'm forty-four years old and I can't get my friends to come out to a norteño dance. When I was doing Padre's, one of the things that I was trying to do was bring in as many norteño and Spanish-language bands as possible. What didn't surprise me so much was that once we started doing those acts on a fairly regular basis, I had much better attendance with those bands than I had for the white bands," David said.

He plays the bass and drums, does vocals, and still plays with some musicians that he played with when he lived in Houston. "We did these Elvis Costello shows in Houston and New Orleans this past weekend. These are all professional musicians that still do it full time. They bring me in every once in a while to do special stuff," David said. Out of thirty-one songs, he sang half of them without playing another instrument. "Just sang lead because the music was somewhat strenuous and complex. On the other sixteen songs I played the bass and sang a little bit of backups. It was a pretty polished show. We actually put out a double CD at the same time."

David wonders whether this musical tradition will stay alive. Hector, the leader of Renacer del Norte, has a nine-year-old son who sits in on rehearsals and takes it all in. "I was a history major at UT and I specialized in Texas, Mexican, and US history. I'm always looking at it like how much longer does this last, this oral history being passed down?" he said.

Tim Thayer and Tom Lehr

Tom Lehr grew up outside Washington, DC, began playing the guitar as a child, and then started playing bass after college. He played in what he calls a "semi post-punk" band before he moved to Marathon. Tom didn't expect to be in a band in Marathon, but Tim Thayer's brother Ted decided to start a band called the Depot Boys because he owned the depot where they rehearsed. Tim came out to Marathon periodically to spend a few months and was the drummer for the band. They played in Monahans, Sanderson, and other small towns in the area. "He and I kind of clicked as a rhythm section. So we've been like the rhythm section ever since then," Tom said.

"We've been a team in different bands, very different bands. Sometimes I'll be playing with a band that he's not playing with. He's playing with a band that I'm not playing with. We've been a team for quite a while," Tim said.

Tim grew up in Houston surrounded by music at home. His mother was a jazz singer but could not pursue it professionally because she had seven children.

"She had a lot of good music. Why I wanted to play drums, I don't know. She had a lot of Caribbean music, a lot of congas, and when I was fifteen, I wanted a surfboard or a set of drums. My dad gave me a hundred and fifty dollars, and the stores were a block apart. I walked back and forth between them. I ended up buying the drums," said Tim. His brothers were musicians, playing the saxophone and clarinet. There was always rock and roll on the radio. "I got into the sixties psychedelic bands, grunge bands, and then I got into Latin music. I married a woman from Mexico and got into that world for a long time in Houston. I played in a conjunto band for ten years," he said. The band, Los Tipos, played rock and roll and also played in Mexican dance halls.

Tim finds the advantage in playing the drums to be that he does not have to know the chords. So when he is called to come and play, he can show up to play just knowing the structure. "I can do that a lot easier than Tom can, a guitar player can. Anyway, I'd get a call: 'Can you come play with this conjunto out of the Valley and play with them for a week?' I learned a lot," he said. Two of the conjunto bands Tim played with in the 1980s were Los Suspiros del Norte and Los Regionales del Valle, a band that played from eight o'clock in the evening until five in the morning. "I fell in with some other musicians where I had to learn music. I still don't read music, but I know music. I had to learn a lot of different music," Tim said. "I've tried to learn to read it. I just don't get it."

Tom and Tim both grew up with Beatles music, and Tim listened to the Cajun radio stations in Houston. Tom studied classical music on the flute for a while but changed his perspective on popular music. "When I was in my late twenties I met a guy who was five years older than me. He said he hated the Beatles. I was stunned because he was the generation that were big Beatles fans. I had him explain it to me. He said that the Beatles killed American music. Because when the British invasion came it was like all the American people were trying to pretend they were English to copy the English guys who were playing American

Tom Lehr (*left*) and Tim Thayer.

music," Tom said. "I started to go back and listen more to the kind of music that was happening before the Beatles. I was familiar with Elvis and Jerry Lee Lewis growing up, but then once the Beatles hit it was all Beatles." He also became more familiar with R&B and soul music, which he had not paid attention to when he was younger. When he moved to Marathon because of the land and landscape, he was listening to Memphis soul and other genres. The major change Tom and Tim see is that there are very few venues left in Marathon, but they do not see much change in the music. "Nothing changes out here very fast, that's one of the good things out here. What we were playing twenty years ago, fifteen years ago, pretty much the same stuff," Tim said.

The number of gigs has diminished in the past year. They were playing with a younger man who lived in the area for a few years and worked on a ranch, who wrote original country songs. When he moved back to Abilene, their gigs were in that area of Texas. Then, they had three or four gigs a month, but now it is one or two every couple of months.

Tom and Tim both sing but insist they are not really singers. "I sing a lot more than I used to. The last band we had, a rock and roll band for a year, year and a half, none of us were singers so we all had to just step in and take over things," said Tim. "None of us were real vocalists, and it's like, 'Do you want to do this song? Well, you're going to sing it.' I was doing a Dwight Yoakam song. I shouldn't have been singing Dwight Yoakam, but it's a good song and nobody else would do it." Tim speaks fluent Spanish but finds he doesn't get to perform much in Spanish. "I sing a hundred good old Mexican songs. Nobody out here does anymore. I don't get to play that anymore unless I'm playing with Tom," Tim said.

Tim Thayer.

"It's the old-school stuff. We had a local band for a while, Latino band, that played a lot of that," said Tom. "One reason norteño music isn't played in Marathon is the lack of accordion players. There used to be horn bands, but they are no longer there. There isn't a school band anymore, either."

"I'm frustrated out here, musically, because I play congas and percussion. I don't ever get to do that anymore except occasionally. And in Houston, there were orchestras and there were Cuban and Colombian salsa bands, and you just don't get that out here," said Tim. Occasionally when he plays with Rick Ruiz of Alpine, he plays congas and enjoys that opportunity.

They had a band called Target Altuda, named for the small, abandoned railroad building by the side of the road with the Target logo painted on its side, reminiscent of the *Prada Marfa* art installation outside Valentine. "The story is, Altuda used to be a town between here and Alpine in the past. Nothing left there except the little railroad building that's no longer in use.

Tom Lehr.

One night, somebody went over there and put a Target sign on it. So the little Target store is like an answer to *Prada Marfa*. So we named our band after that because a couple of us were here in Marathon and one of us was in Alpine so it was just kind of halfway," said Tom.

In spite of the lack of venues in Marathon, they do play weddings in the area. Since the population of Marathon is growing, that may increase the demand for live music. Tim builds houses and says there are more new houses being built than he has ever seen.

"It's retired people. There was another couple without children, but a younger couple, professionals, who work online. There are more people with kids moving here. The population of the school has increased," he said. However, one drawback to older people moving to town is the lack of extensive health care. "You get a lot of people that this is their part-time home, their second home. They'll come out and stay for a few weeks and then go back to San Antonio or Houston and live there," said Tim.

Tom plans to stay in Marathon permanently, but Tim would like to move back to the Texas coast, maybe Port Aransas. First, however, he needs to finish building his own house in order to sell it. He is tired of the desert. "I'm the water man and I fish. It's good out here, it's been very good for me. It's been good for my life. A lot of good things that I needed to happen, happened. But as far as the physical environment, it's dry. If I wanted to hike and climb mountains it would be great," Tim said.

"So, you've been waiting ten years for a guitar player to move to town and now you say you're going to move away," Tom laughs.

David Arnold

David Arnold lives in Alpine. He moved there in 1961 at the age of five. His father was a pharmacist and opened the Prescription Shoppe in town.

No one in David's family was a musician. He grew up listening to big band music, and Dean Martin was a favorite of his mother. The first album his parents owned was by Benny Goodman. His cousin listened to Motown, causing David to want to be a musician. He did not know the individual artists but liked the sound. He had older half brothers who grew up in Iraan, a small town in Pecos County, and other small oil field towns. "There were always these bands that would get together and some of them became kind of famous. For instance, there was Roy Orbison from Wink and Buddy Holly. My oldest brother, Tom, used to talk about going to high school dances and hearing those guys when they were first starting out. I think that influenced me a little bit too. I always looked up to him," David said.

All the way through high school, David played the cornet in the school band. He was also teaching himself to play the guitar. His father bought one for his sister, but David ended up playing it. "It was a Silvertone and it had the amp built into the case and also it came with a record album, *Learn to Play the Guitar with Adventures*. I tried to get through that the best I could. I was already learning how to read music in the band," he said.

David had a band in junior high called the Gingerbread Militia and in high school played for school dances with Israfel, a three-piece band with a guitar, drums, and a bass. "In 1972 or '73, we decided Rush would be a great name for our band. So we were Rush. We're out in West Texas and we don't know about Rush. This guy shows up with their first album, and we listened to it and we knew we couldn't be Rush," David said. They performed in the surrounding towns including Fort Stockton, Marfa, Fort Davis, and Grand Falls all through high school. They would not play any country music at all. They played Jimi Hendrix, Deep Purple, and ZZ Top: hard rock in an area where this was not played on local radio.

Their first paying gig was for the all-school prom in Presidio and the whole student body of fifty came. The band members had to be driven by their mothers to Presidio because none of them were old enough to drive. There were seven band members at the time and David played guitar. A unique feature of their performance was reminiscent of the rain chants at Woodstock; they would pass out percussion instruments such as tambourines and claves to the audience. Everyone would be involved in the performance.

The number of band members changed. Their first vocalist was the son of the local Baptist preacher, so he had to keep his singing with the band a secret. The bass player decided to quit and then there were three members: David, another bass player, and drummer Charlie Hill. David was voted bass player and lead vocalist by the remaining band members. He didn't have a bass and they had a looming gig in Monahans for the youth fellowship program at a church. There wasn't much time to learn the songs, much less find a bass. The musician who was lending the instrument to the band decided he did not want David to play it. "I was getting pretty nervous about it. The deadline was coming up and I went to Bloys Encampment that

David Arnold.

summer and went to where they have youth fellowship and music. There was a guy playing a copy of a Fender Hofner Beatle bass and I prayed to God, 'Oh, God. I need a bass. I need a bass. I'd love to have one like that. Oh, please, God. I'd like a real one.' You know, praying away for this. I really got into the spirit of it," David said. His prayers were answered when two weeks later there was an ad in the *Alpine Avalanche* listing a Hofner Beatle bass and an amplifier for sale. David's father encouraged him to pursue music and bought the bass and amp for him.

"The next thing I know, I'm standing in front of these kids in Monahans and I'm just scared to death. I went on autopilot and I discovered that I can do two things at once. I can play bass, which is kind of a countermelody, and sing melody over the top of it. It was kind of a do-or-die thing and I was able to do it. So I became a bass player at that point," he said.

They were becoming familiar with the music they wanted to play. Their bass player at the time, Travis Tucker, had an uncle who sent them albums while he was stationed in England. Those albums, by Jimi Hendrix, Cream, Black Flag, and the Hello People, and the album *Super Sessions* had the sound they loved. This music was not being played at all in the Big Bend, so they needed to find a way to get it on the local radio station, which refused to play anything but country and big band music. "It was absolutely the voice of no choice. Then later on, my friend Travis, who had been the bass player in Gingerbread Militia, got a job at the radio station. So, we'd take our albums down there. He had two hours where he could play whatever he wanted and we exposed everybody to this rock music, which really helped Israfel because we were playing some of this music. We really didn't know what the hits were, right? So we played the songs that we liked off the album, not necessarily the ones that made it," said David.

David moved to New Orleans, where his two brothers lived, and spent time at Preservation Hall in 1975, hearing new and varied music, including that of Leon Redbone. One musician who came in to jam was Jon Bon Jovi. "I'd been in there one night and Pete Fountain comes in and he starts playing and man, he took everybody down the street to his place. Al Hirt used to do this thing," said David.

After living in Houston for a while, David returned to Alpine and started playing guitar again in another rock band that included one of the original members of the Gingerbread Militia. They played at the Granada while it was still a theater with a stage and first-class acoustics.

We are having lunch at Reata, which David remembers from when it used to be Downtown Brown's Restaurant and Bar. "It belonged to Randy and Mary Lynn Brown, who were musicians from Dallas. They played with a lot of these big classic country stars that would come in. They would play on the weekends. I picked up a bass-playing gig with them. They played with Rio Grande, a country band they were in for a while. We played in that. And a film crew was down here filming one of the *Lonesome Dove* movies. The crew loved this place. They came down on Friday and Saturday nights and we just had the best ol' time," David said. When David was performing with Rio Grande, he sang harmonies with Brent Parsons and performed classic country and western.

David has performed from El Paso to Junction, Colorado, and for the Marfa dance clubs. "They loved us, especially when I had Charlie in the band playing drums because this power trio guy is playing country and we got a beat," said David.

Our server, Betsy Stevens Pauls, went to high school with David and remembers their bands, including Spontaneous Combustion. "I think that was forty-something years ago. Their band was primarily the same guys who were playing until seven or eight years ago. Maybe sooner than that when one of the band members passed. Charlie played the drums up until he couldn't. He was sick. The last time he played it was very hard on him but he gave it all he could," said Betsy.

David no longer performs. "My last gig was the last gig Betsy talked about that Charlie Hill played at the Railroad Blues. I think that was three or four years ago. I've done it kind of out of respect for Charlie. The fact that he was such a good drummer and we were on such a good wavelength, it's hard to re-create that with other people," David said.

Steve Bennack

Steve Bennack was born in the Rio Grande Valley, in Raymondville, Texas, fifty miles north of Brownsville. He and his family moved to Alpine when he was eleven years old. He was fifteen or sixteen when he decided that he wanted to make his living as a musician. "I started piano lessons when I was six, in the first grade. I picked up the guitar and got serious about it about the time I started the seventh grade, which was because I saw Dave and Charlie and Steve, they were already playing in bands, and it was like, man, these guys are cool," he said.

He began playing the trombone in his junior high band, then during his freshman year, he began playing tuba and could already play electric bass. "My senior year in high school, there was a professor here, Dr. Earl Gay, who started a chamber orchestra. So, I learned how to play the upright bass and how to play orchestral bass," Steve said. When he first started playing the guitar he learned the cowboy chords from his father's Tony Mottola chord book, then he started listening to Chuck Berry. "My brother bought me a copy of *Led Zeppelin II* for Christmas and it was one of those things where I burned out the grooves on some of those albums. Lift the tone arm, move it back, listen to it again," he said.

He earned his undergraduate degree at Sul Ross, pursued a master's in music theory at the University of North Texas, and received his master of liberal arts degree from Sul Ross in 2004. He has been teaching at Sul Ross since 1995 except for a couple of years working construction with David Arnold and teaching

Steve Bennack at Sul Ross State University.

private music lessons. He is a part-time adjunct professor. "When I enjoy it the most is when I have students that really want to learn. I mean, that's what makes it enjoyable," he said.

Although he did not play country-western with David Arnold in Spontaneous Combustion, they all did play country later. When they played with Brent Parsons, it was a mix of rock, country, and a wide variety of music. Brent came back to play a benefit for Charlie Hill when he was ill and surprised the audience with their first song. "It was just like we had played a gig last weekend. It was funny because everybody had always seen us play rock and roll and expected

Steve Bennack.

hard rock and we start out with "Two Dollars in the Jukebox." Some people didn't like it," Steve said.

Steve sees the change in music in the Big Bend as being due to the bands that come to perform from outside the area. "The single most thing that contributed to that would have been the Railroad Blues: RC Toler and Richard Fallon, because Richard had been involved in music and had been in bands, I think in Baton Rouge and Austin. Richard definitely had connections with people in Austin for bringing Austin bands here. You know, they developed it into a well-known venue," Steve said. The band used to perform frequently in Terlingua at La Kiva and played in Presidio twice, but Steve thought they were lucky to have the Railroad Blues as their local venue.

David Arnold and the drummer Charlie Hill had known each other as children. "They had a band about 1969. It was called the Unknowns. I think Steve probably started playing with them maybe about 1972 or something like that. I was hanging around them, kind of a hanger-on and we'd get together and jam. Steve (Cowell) and I and his brother Jeff, and this other guy Harlan were in the first rock band, a garage band when I was a freshman in high school. What brought Spon Com around was that it turned out that we were all living here again from various places," Steve said. He had lived in Austin three different times in the years since he had left Alpine. His father was a retired physician in general practice in town and he hired Steve to help him build a house for his retirement. He stayed.

While Steve was gone, Alpine changed. More people have moved to town, since they can work remotely by computer. The music scene has expanded as well. In the past he and David and Charlie would jam at a bar called the Cross Country—which is gone now, replaced by a Subway—and it was an event that drew crowds. "Things have really changed in that respect as far as how many different choices you have now in venues, certainly a lot more choices. A lot more groups playing and more places to see them,

that's probably the biggest change as far as the music goes," Steve said.

When Charlie Hill passed away, both David and Steve keenly felt the loss. They had played together for years and they were friends. Their connection both on and off the stage is what drew people to their performances. Steve Cowell would come to Alpine a few times a year from Austin and they would perform together. "We'd get together and play and knock the rust off. We weren't what you'd call a polished band because every gig was a reunion gig, until Charlie got sick and then we did some benefit gigs to raise money for him while he was still able to play the drums," Steve said. "Amazing how long he was still able to play the drums. Up until maybe about three or four months before he passed away. We'd known each other for so long, the chemistry that we had between each other, people could tell that we weren't just guys in a band. We were guys that had been friends for a long, long time."

Spontaneous Combustion performed from 1991 until Charlie passed away at the end of 2013. They were the first hard rock band in the Big Bend, playing the music of the late 1960s and 1970s. Later, another band, Freedom's Conquest, with Robert Halpern as the drummer, played some hard rock as well. Before Steve joined Spon Com, David, Charlie, and Steve Cowell, among others, performed as Gingerbread Militia.

No other band in the Big Bend now performs music from the late 1960s to 1970s. The younger bands perform music from the 1980s and 1990s. Since Marfa has the reputation of being the center of the arts in the Big Bend, venues there attract the widest variety of music. "They get a lot of music performances in there. Everything from classical to multimedia modern. They've certainly had some things over there I'm sure where they had DJs and things like that," said Steve.

He still performs occasionally with Tom Lehr and Tim Thayer of Marathon, although those gigs have decreased in the past year.

Stephen Cowell holds his eight-string Dobro.

Stephen Cowell

Stephen Cowell and his brother Jeff are the older brothers of Shanna Cowell of the JUGS. Their family lived in Euless and Hurst. Shanna was born in Sweetwater and Jeff was born in Alpine. Their father earned a degree in civil engineering and technology and worked as a city manager.

Stephen came from Austin to be interviewed. He is a computer programmer and a firmware engineer for Semiconductor Support Services. "It is like the software that goes inside of chips. The internet of things. Your toaster talks to your refrigerator talks to your router and they order from the grocery store. I'm involved in that kind of stuff. My company supports wafer fab equipment, which is the maker of chips. So I'm using chips to work on equipment that makes chips," he explained. Stephen says his company's opportunities are in obsolete equipment that people want to keep using. "They've got CRT monitors with light-pen control and you can't use cathode ray tube TV-style stuff anymore, so our first patent was the replacement for the CRT to use an electromagnetic pen. We took those monitors and used them to replace a light pen on a control for a tool. We sell thousands of those every year," he said. "We replaced the floppy disks with a box that has SD cards in it and is also on the internet. You can move files on and off the tool using the internet instead of flip a floppy. This is big, people love this stuff. They love their old machines and we keep those machines running and updated. It's a great company to work for and it's a great position. I get to feel creative."

He began playing the guitar at the age of eight in 1967 on a little acoustic guitar with a crack in it that his mother bought for him for eleven dollars. "My uncle David ended up being forced to give me an old Japanese electric and a RadioShack amplifier. That was my first electric, I got that in '69," he said. The family moved back to Alpine in 1970 and he began playing with the junior high students. That was when Gingerbread Militia was formed with David Arnold,

Travis Tucker, Charlie Hill, and Stephen, with others joining and leaving. "That was about the time I got my first good electric guitar. I was hanging out at my grandmother's and just poking around as kids do and I went and looked under a bed and found my uncle's first Fender electric guitar. It was a Duo Sonic II, made in 1965, and those are actually interesting guitars. They were only made for one or two years. So, I found that. I didn't ask. I just took it," Stephen said. That guitar belonged to his uncle David, who was Stephen's musical inspiration. His uncle began the band Links, later changed to Lynx, reflecting a change in the music they performed, going from the Beatles to hard rock. The band moved to Dallas and became well known. "I went and saw them in Odessa in the seventies when they were out touring around. He was always an idol, that's one of the reasons I think I wanted to play electric guitar," he said. Stephen remembers that while listening to his uncle's band perform, his love for music ignited. "The band had a giant double bass with a Marshall stack and a wall of three hundred fifteen custom bass amps. It's super loud but it doesn't hurt. You're just soaking it in. It's just like pleasant noise and I can feel the legs of my pants vibrating. That's probably what hooked me on rock and roll music," Stephen said.

When the decision was made to form Spontaneous Combustion, they needed instruments. Their first drum set was sparkly orange. "Charlie beat the crap out of that drum set, but then we found a set of wonderful Rogers drums at the Wool & Mohair Barn, the local consignment house," Stephen said. After they outfitted it with cymbals, they had a good drum set. Then, a Hammond organ became available at the Wool Barn. "It was only six hundred bucks for a 1952 B2 with a Leslie cabinet Hammond organ. So we got that thing and took it apart. There was a dead rat in the Leslie. Stuck under the woofer. We got that out, cleaned it all up, and did a lot of work to it, and it's an electro-mechanical wonder," he said. Stephen is very knowledgeable about Hammond organs. He explains that they have electronics and mechanics. "The notes on a guitar, electric guitar, there's a pickup and the string vibrates and breaks the magnetic field. There's something like that inside a Hammond organ. There's a wheel. It's called a tone wheel. It's like a saw blade and it's turning and it goes past a magnetic pickup. So a Hammond organ is very similar to an electric guitar with the vacuum tubes and everything, to make the sound that it makes," Stephen said. He believes the Hammond organ, and Steve Bennack playing it, made the band sound good.

They realized none of them could sing as well as they wanted to, so they all learned how to sing and play at the same time. When Richard Fallon moved to town, they found their singer. When Richard became part owner of Railroad Blues, they also had their venue.

Stephen moved back to Alpine in 1989, and then Michael Stevens came to town in 1990 and opened his guitar store. "We thought we had died and gone to heaven because you could only get guitar strings at the drugstore and they were Black Diamond acoustic strings. There was no music store. You had to order, mail order, or go to Odessa or El Paso to buy music stuff. I could walk into Mike's shop and see an Eric Johnson '54 Stratocaster, or Junior Brown's red guit-steel, or any number of beautiful instruments that he's made for rich people everywhere," he said.

Stephen switched from playing the guitar with a pick to playing with his fingers. He realized that would give him a muting technique. That led to him playing the slide guitar. "Once you get the muting technique on the slide guitar, regular old Allman Brothers–type slide guitar gets a lot easier because you've got the muting in the right hand down. Then I started putting the guitar in tunings instead of E-A-D-G-B-D, you'd put it in an E chord or an A chord or something like that to make it easier to play blues," Stephen said. He thought it was awkward and decided to get a steel guitar. Stephen shows us an eight-string Dobro tuned to E-13, a steel guitar tuning called a swing or western swing tuning. He owns fifteen lap steel guitars and a few Dobros. He recently sold a pedal steel guitar, noted for being difficult to play. "It's the theater organ of guitar. You have pedals, you have knee levers. There's ten strings on two necks. There's a volume pedal, which your right foot is always supposed to be doing. That's the most important part of a steel guitar is the volume pedal. You've got knee levers that your right knee is supposed to be doing. And if you switch necks you have to move your left knee from one set of knee levers to the other. I'm just amazed that people actually manage to play the pedal steel guitar as well as they do," Stephen said. Currently, he does not play as much electric guitar anymore, concentrating on lap steel and the eight-string Dobro.

He has an upcoming event in Dallas at the Texas Steel Guitar Association Jamboree. He runs the nonpedal room that frequently features older players who began on lap steel. They are allowed to record videos that can be seen on Stephen's YouTube channel.

The death of Charlie Hill, the drummer of Spon Com, marked the end of the band, since none of them can imagine the band without him. Stephen thinks that if they ever tried to perform again together, it would have to be in something other than their original band.

"I don't hardly listen to music at all," Stephen said, "because all I have to do is think in my head and I can drop the needle on 'A Whole Lotta Love.' It's a part of me."

Scott Walker

Born in Houston, Scott Walker left there after he discovered the Big Bend on his high school senior trip. "I had not been to the Big Bend before. I was already committed to attend my freshman year at Sam Houston so I did that, but I got here as quick as I could and I came to Sul Ross. I was here for my college years and then I moved to northeast Texas where my father had a ranch near Mineola, north of Tyler," he said.

He took care of the ranch for nearly thirty years but also played a lot of music during that time. His father was a musician and played the guitar and the piano. He gave Scott his first music lesson and he learned something very valuable about playing music. "My first lesson, he played a C chord and said, 'How does that make you feel?' Then he played a C minor and said, 'What does that make you feel like?' I said, 'It's kind of sad.' And he played a seventh chord and he said, 'How does that make you feel?' 'I don't know. Silly. A silly chord.' And so that was my first introduction to how the chords . . . it's a feeling thing. It's an emotion. And I think that was such a great gift that he gave me from the very beginning. How music provokes and is tied to emotion," Scott said.

Scott had a small honky-tonk band in high school and his two band members are still performing today in Houston and Austin. He began writing songs and performing in bands. Scott and his father started a small recording studio in northeast Texas.

He learned to play guitar in his twenties while living in Alpine. "There was a guy that used to come pick me up at my house on Sundays. Old biker guy. We'd go over to a little burned out place next to the Toltec bar over there. It was just all burned out and caved in but we'd go out to the back and there were these old Mexican men playing guitar. I would sit in and if you'd make a move they'd give you a hard look. Not your turn yet. It was weeks. Warren would pick me up and take me out there and we would nod at each other and then finally one of these guys nodded at me, 'It's your turn.' But the whole time I was studying and watching what they're doing. I got a cool influence there. In the eighties and in the nineties there was a lot more of that influence here because you could cross the border. There were dances down here all the time," he said.

Scott thinks the reason there are not as many dances is because the clubs do not pay much, and the musicians may make as little as fifty or sixty dollars for a performance. Given the long distances to drive to a gig in the Big Bend, that would just cover gas money. "It would be nice to profit from this. In 2010 I had been playing in different bands. I'd played in

Scott Walker.

Larry Joe Taylor's band for a couple of years and that led to a lot of great side gigs and playing with a lot of people. I got to play with Joe Ely and Rusty Wier, these guys were my heroes," he said. He went out on his own as a songwriter and found that to be much harder. "After riding on a tour bus and making pretty decent money, going back and gigging in my car was hard. My gigs really dried up and I said, 'I'm not going to play music anymore. Forget this. Everybody out here is being taken advantage of and I'm tired of it and it's not worth it for me anymore to play music professionally,'" Scott said.

He became a long-distance trucker for a few years but still wrote songs in the back of his truck. He did not have a professional musician's presence since he unplugged from social media. "My wife the whole time has kept me relevant. Posting her things that she posts. But really I had gotten to a point that I said I'm just not going to play because I can't feed my family. I can't make enough money. And I've been doing this all my life. I started off making a hundred, a hundred and fifty dollars a night in high school. I should be doing better than that these days," he said. Scott decided since he had spent a lot of his adult life dedicated to music, he would do it for fun if he could not make a living. For the past ten years he has played pickup gigs and sat in on jams. Now that he is recording a new CD, he has found his passion again.

Scott and two partners have bought the old Frontier Dance Hall, closed for fifteen years. "It was the local place for people to go. For years, the Frontier was the thing. Now, I have some partners and we're opening the old dance hall back up. I'm going to put in an outdoor stage. We're going to make this a music venue. We're fifty miles south of Alpine. We can attract Alpine people. We can certainly get in on this Viva Big Bend festival that they're doing. Next year I hope that we are able to participate in that. My plan, long term, is over the next ten years, develop my fan base and bring them to a festival. I plan to have three festivals a year at the Frontier. It's time," Scott said. He is also building

a recording studio that he hopes will attract musicians from Austin as well as the Big Bend.

Terlingua Ranch is where Scott and his wife make their home. They bought a place that needed a lot of work, and Scott is a skilled electrician, plumber, and construction worker. "I've done this all my life. It's as if all of my life experiences have led me to this place where I am now," he said. Scott sees big changes coming to the Big Bend, particularly the Terlingua Ranch area. "It is people my age that are moving out here and we're bringing resources and we're working hard to build things. I have been three years working on the infrastructure of my place. I have probably the largest water catchment in Brewster County. I have a sixty-five-thousand gallon rainwater tank that is full of water and it pressurizes my entire valley. I have my own water treatment plant that I built myself. We're coming out and doing it right and doing it big. We're not living in a shack made of pallets," Scott said. He has been in Terlingua for three years and has found that the isolation and the quiet have caused him to be overwhelmed by the noise and people in nearby cities like Midland-Odessa and El Paso. His son, now twenty-five, came to live in Terlingua but left after a year because he found it too isolated.

Scott has had difficulty finding labor to help with his land. He has his own concrete mixing plant and mixes his own concrete. "All of us are self-sustained, self-contained, so that's the changes that I see coming to Terlingua is that younger people are bringing resources and really establishing a presence here," he said. Now it is much less difficult to live in Terlingua with Amazon, UPS delivery, and even some Airbnbs for rent.

Scott notes that previously in Terlingua, the town was mostly off the grid, but now internet service has been added and more people live there. "It used to be a ghost town. People squatting in the ruins. That was my favorite. You'd go out and just start playing guitar and people just wander up and the most amazing magic happened down there when it was like that," Scott said.

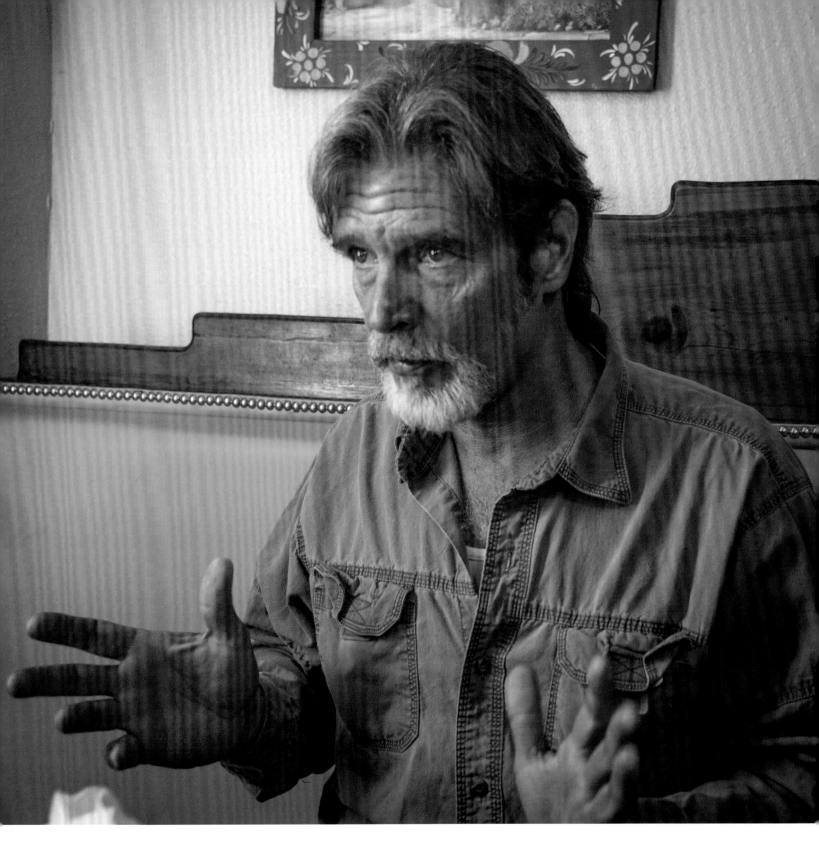

The influence from the music of Mexico changed after the border closed, Scott believes. "If you get caught up in the Terlingua thing and you hang out here for a few months and find yourself derailed in Terlingua like many musicians do, sure, you're going to pick up on those influences. Absolutely. But I think nothing is like it was. When they closed the border it changed drastically. It changed our interaction with the Mexican culture. It used to be, just cross. You just cross. It was just a little river. And then we had our dances and we had our fun. Now, you can't do that anymore." The High Sierra restaurant in Terlingua had to close its kitchen because the entire staff was deported. The kitchen workers had gone across the river to a funeral and were picked up by the Border Patrol when they returned.

The people who choose to make their home in an isolated area like the Big Bend embrace a distinctly nonurban way of life. There are none of the traffic jams, crowds, Walmarts, or pollution typical of big-city life. There is change taking place, however. "It's a very scary time in America right now. Everyone is so divided," Scott says. "Many of them are taking a side that is not defensible. It's untenable. It's unsustainable. What are you trying to do to our world? You guys are getting way too caught up in this. You're not seeing reality," Scott said.

11

Songs from Both Sides

Reina de Mi Amor (Queen of My Love)
By Sunny Ozuna

Tu eres la reina de mi amor
Tu eres la reina de mi vida
Y sabes que te quiero, todavia
Aunque me hagas llorar

Hombres, no deben de llorar
Pero te vengo llorando
Tu eres la reina de mi amor . . . reina de mi amor. . .

Sin ti, yo no puedo vivir . . . (chorus)
Yo no puedo existir
Por lo tanto que te quiero
Contigo, me siento como un rey
Pero sin ti mejor me muero.

(*Repeat song from beginning*)

(By permission of Ildefonso "Sunny" Ozuna)

Smile Now, Cry Later

Smile now, cry later,
Smile now, cry later, for you . . . for you

My friends tell me, you could never belong to me
So I'll smile for my friends and cry later . . .
Smile now, cry later,
Smile now, cry later . . . for you . . . for you

I wouldn't be crying, if I didn't love you so
I'll smile for my friends and cry later,
Smile for my friends and cry later . . . for you . . . for you

(ad lib) Tell that you love me, that you put nobody else above me
That you cross your heart

(By permission of Ildefonso "Sunny" Ozuna)

If Old Hats Could Talk

"If that old hat could talk
Why the tales that it could spin"
Of old cowboy hats I've heard that said
Time and time again

Down in the brush country of south Texas
Where Frank Dobie used to roam
Where the cattle feed on prickly pear
And the rattlesnake's right at home

You'll find the little town of Cotulla
And a Front Street store called Ben's
Where a bunch of old hats hang on the wall
Once worn by local cowmen

When city folks walk through the door
They can't believe their eyes
These greasy, dirty, beat up hats
Are displayed like a prize

Each hat has a personality
Like the man it once adorned
Shaped by time and weather
Creased by wind, and brush, and thorn

My favorite is Piggy Jenkins' hat
He's now crossed that Great Divide
But his old sombrero's easy to spot
Cause it hangs there all cock-eyed

When Piggy would go in to chouse a cow
Out of her black-brush bed
Folks say he'd grab the brim of his hat
And just screw it down on his head

There's hats of fellers young and old
And those gone over to the other side
Hats of Mexican vaqueros
Hang next to those of the bosses for whom they ride

Sometimes early of a morning
With my coffee and the hats I sit alone
And I hear the ring of spur rowels
And the saddles creak and groan

Just think of the many things
Those hats have seen over the years
Children born, loved ones passing
The work, the fun, and the tears

They've worked a million head of cattle
Pulled God knows how many baby calves
Been covered with scours, blood, and stomach chyme
And no telling how many kinds of salve

They could tell of rides on bad ol' broncs
That were determined to swaller their heads
And probably a few tender love stories
From hanging on a four poster bed

They've been used as weapons to swat everything
From charging mamma cows to flies
They've been tipped to ladies, and doffed in honor
When Old Glory was carried by

And how many times did those cowboys say
"Somethin' musta got in my eye"
As they clutched their hat tight to their chest
For a compadre's final good-bye

They've bent to the wind and the speed of a
  good horse
Two stepped and waltzed all night
Heard things these men told only to God
Up on some hill at dawn's first light

I've heard many worldly travelers tell
Of great art galleries where they've been
But to me those paintings can't hold a candle
To the tales these old hats can spin

(By permission of Don Cadden)

Cow Women

Those cowgirls you see in the magazines
They all look pretty and slick
Not a hair out of place, face made up
Lots of sexy pink lipstick

The high-dollar jeans look painted on
To a body with a tight behind
Man made boobs peek out of rhinestone shirts
That'll blow a cowboy's mind

Now the women I work with don't dress like that
But they've all got plenty of sand
These ol' gals are cowboys to the bone
They'll dang sure make you a hand

They can drag a calf on a half broke horse
Or be part of the flankin' crew
They'll take a knife, change a bull to a steer
Then make you some oyster stew

I've seen 'em covered with guacamole
When preg checking time comes around
Then wash up clean in a water trough
And head for the big dance in town

They'll take the outside circle
Busting the brush in a lope
Then put some snot-slingin' cow in the pen
Before you can shake out your rope

If you think "cowboy" is a term of gender
You've been watching too much TV
I've seen women make the kind of hand
Most men just try to be

When those city gals marched for women's lib
They should have come out west
They'd could have learned equality
In muck boots and a Carhartt vest

Our girls look good in their worn out jeans
Packin' a 50 pound bag of cake
Or taking a pistol or long-handled hoe
To a pissed off rattlesnake

So keep your fancy magazines
And the models who set all the trends
Give me a gal with some poop on her boots
And lots of bottom end

(By permission of Don Cadden)

Ballad of Ernesto Galvan

Down south of old San Antone, is a country that God left alone
Where the cactus has thorns, and the deer grow big horns
And the weather is usually warm
Where the coyote howls, and the panther he prowls
And the rattlesnake grows 6 feet long
The people who live there, have always had their share
Of working themselves to the bone

When the sun comes up for the day
He's out saddling up his old bay
He'll ride the mesquite, in the terrible heat
As his father did the same way
He'll rope and he'll brand, it's the law of the land
The cows think they're his, but they're not
He's just earning a buck, 'cause in a new pickup truck
El Jefe sees over the lot

CHORUS:
    Ernesto, Ernesto Galvan, you're truly a man of the land
    You've chased mucha vaca, with caballo and reata
    You're a muy bueno cowhand

Has ridden miles with Ernesto Galvan
The years how they fly, time's passed you by
But you're still one hell of a man

CHORUS:
    He still rides with his dogs by his side
    Remembering the past with great pride
    Didn't make much dinero, for a macho vaquero
    But from his loop the steers could not hide
    When it's time to turn in, and God says my friend
    We're fixing to change your luck
    'Cause in heaven take my word, El Jefe rides herd
    And you get the new pickup truck

CHORUS

(By permission of Don Cadden)

When the Sun Explodes

I've got you like I always do
If you need a friend with a helping hand to lend
I can be there quick to stand like a candlestick
to brighten up the darkened hall leading to where you belong
Then I'll shake your hand, look you in the eye
Tell you it's all right. Leave you with a smile
'til the next time comes that you need someone
that you know won't go, when the bad winds blow
and your spirit's low

And when the sun explodes and away we go
Will the past survive past the speed of time
And the day run away with night
The night become the light
Will I find you there blown beyond all care

From sea to sea winning little victories
From breath to breath, dying a little death
I'll be lonesome too and if you want me to
I'll hear the tears you shed, see the blood you bled
Then I'll shake your hand, look you in the eye
Tell me what you see. Would you remember me?
When the next time comes that I need someone
That I know won't fly if I stand aside
And I start to cry.

And when the sun explodes and away we go
Will the past survive past the speed of time
And the day run away with the night
The night becomes the light
Will I find you there blown beyond all care

When the next time comes that we see someone
It will have been a long dark while and a million miles
Since we've seen a smile.

(By permission of Chris McWilliams)

Saguaro

By Michael Stevens

The daylight was a slippin'
through the mountains to the East
He grabbed his guns and he mounted up,
he was off, to say the least
He rode along in silence,
a chill was in the air
The monsters had to be cut down
or they'd soon be everywhere

Saguaro . . . a menace to the West!

His name was David Grundman
a noxious little twerp
He saw the giant plants as the Clanton gang
and himself as Wyatt Earp
So he drove out to the desert—
they wouldn't come to town
Out in Maricopa County
He vowed to shoot them down

Saguaro . . . a menace to the West!

He strode up to the first one
not the largest of the lot
With a lightning move he sidestepped
and killed him with one shot
When the smoke had cleared, the cactus
had lost that final round
Two hundred years of nature's work
lay splattered on the ground

(small fandango clap clap) Hey Ho!

He crossed a small arroyo
the sun was in his eyes
He was looking for the leader
he'd know him by his size
When all at once upon a ridge
the squinting gunman saw
Twenty-seven feet of succulent
challenging his draw

Saguaro . . . a menace to the West!

He was slightly disadvantaged
by the angle of the sun
But after all the cactus
wasn't packing any gun
His finger twitched, he made his move
he drew, his guns did bark
and echoed with his laughter
as the bullets hit their mark

Now the mighty cactus trembled
then came the warning sound
One mighty arm of justice
came hurtling toward the ground
The gunman staggered backward,
he whimpered and he cried
The Saguaro . . . crushed him like a bug
and David Grundman died

Saguaro . . . a menace to the West

David Grundman . . . a menace to the West

The End

(By permission of Michael Stevens)

Ozymandias

By Gary Oliver

He come out to the badlands, seen 'em as an
    empty slate
He didn't know just what he'd build, but he knew
    it would be great
And anyone got in his way, he'd crush 'em or
    he'd buy
'Cause he had to build a Xanadu underneath
    the desert sky.

All he needed was
H – 2 – O
There's enough here for our children
H – 2 – O
It's a better day that's coming soon
H – 2 – O
There's water, water everywhere for to make this
    desert bloom.

2. They laughed at Will and Orville when they
    brought the gift of flight
They laughed at old Tom Edison when he blessed
    their dark with light
They laugh when anyone with will and vision
    dares to shoot the moon
They laughed at 'em, they're laughing now,
    but they'll be crying soon,

When they see our
H – 2 – O
In pools and lakes and fountains
H – 2 – O
In waves a-rolling on these sands
H – 2 – O
Cascading down our mountains
Now, nothing lasts forever, so let's enjoy it
    while we can.

3. There's folks out there with money, just wondering
    where to go
They've played in Monte Carlo, skied in Aspen
    through the snow
They've sailed the seas, seen the islands, done it
    all before
Now they want to golf our Last Frontier 'fore they
    reach that other shore.

So thank you
H – 2 – O
This surf machine's a winner
H – 2 – O
Let's take our drinks down by the pool
H – 2 – O
It'll be jet skis after dinner,
Fly-fishing by the waterfall where the air's so fresh
    and cool.

4. There's excursions in the desert, where all life
    hangs by a thread
You can shoot your own coyote, mount a
    javelina's head
ATV down by the riverbed, where once the
    water ran
Take a postcard shot of poverty out across the
    Rio Grande,

Where there's no more
H – 2 – O
It was nice but now it's over
H – 2 – O
Now it all belongs to someone else
H – 2 – O
Thank God for all these policemen
Or else they'd slip across that border, take our
    water for themselves.

5. When the roll is called up yonder, when the final
   trumpet sounds
   When they line up by the Pearly Gates, and the
   angels gather 'round
   Counting who's been bad and who's been good
   and if there's any blame
   Y' better hope that God's a golfer, or else you're
   headed for the flames.

   Gonna need a lotta
   H – 2 – O
   Used to be so much around here
   H – 2 – O
   But now this desert never ends
   H – 2 – O
   Geology takes over
   Wait 500 million years or so, build a new resort
   again.
   Wait 500 million years or so,
   Build a new resort
   Again.

   (By permission of Gary Oliver)

Valentine (polka)
By Gary Oliver

I come to town, the sun was high
The wind was down, the creek was dry,
Licked my finger, stuck it up
I felt inclined to try my luck.
I met a gal out for a stroll,
So pretty, just a little bold.
She looked me up, she looked me down.
Folks sure are friendly in this town.

Take me back to Valentine, I'm not ready for Alpine,
Where whiskey flows down streets of sin—
Oh, what a mess it's got me in.
Take me back to Valentine, I had a dollar and a dime.
Now that's all gone, this Brewster crowd,
They'll chew you up and spit you out.

2. The sun went down, the lights come out,
   Saloons and gin mills all about
   The whiskey fog, the neon glare,
   The golden ringlets in her hair.
   I'm not sure where it all went wrong
   One minute I's dancing in the throng,
   The next, I woke in pain and hurt,
   My pockets empty, in the dirt.

   Take me back to Valentine, I'm not ready for Alpine,
   Where whiskey flows down streets of sin—
   Oh, what a mess it's got me in.
   Take me back to Valentine, I had a dollar and a dime.
   Now that's all gone, this Brewster crew,
   They'll kick you down and laugh at you.

3. Went to the law to seek redress, found myself
      under arrest.
   They put me on the highway gang, pouring asphalt,
      wearing chains
   A car sped by, we ate the dust, while golden ringlets
      waved at us
   They laughed, threw bottles, then were gone,
   We'd clean their highway later on.

   Take me back to Valentine, I'm not ready for
      Alpine,
   Where whiskey flows down streets of sin—
   Oh, what a mess it's got me in.
   Take me back to Valentine, I had a dollar and
      a dime.
   Now that's all gone, this Brewster gang,
   They'll come at you with tooth and fang.

4. I work till dusk, rise at dawn—my waking
      moments ain't my own
   But when my mind does drift and roam, I think of
      folks far from this farm.
   Some dark night I'll steal away, move by night and
      hide by day—
   Find the highway, paint a sign, says Take Me Back
      to Valentine.

   Take me back to Valentine, I'm not ready for
      Alpine,
   Where whiskey flows down streets of sin—
   Oh, what a mess it's got me in.
   Take me back to Valentine, I had a dollar and
      a dime.
   Now that's all gone, this Brewster crowd,
   They'll chew you up and spit you out.
   So please stop when you see my sign,
   Take me back to Valentine.

(By permission of Gary Oliver)

Dinosaur Song for Max – A Modern Boy

Words and music by Ray Freese

Two hundred twenty-five million years ago, or so
Long before your mom and dad were born
Lived a creature that we now call dinosaur
Not a fiery dragon or a foolish unicorn
This one lived in the Pangea swamps
In fact that was his home
Throughout most of history
He was free to roam

Then there came Max
The latest link in evolution's chain Max
Things will never be the same
You're the first and last
The future and the past—Max

These gentle giants weighed in at eighty tons or so
They were even taller than your house
They ate all their fruits and nuts and vegetables
And would not even harm a mouse-or-us
Your ancestors were friends of theirs
In the same time and place
They evolved to be the heirs we now call the human
    race

Then there came Max
The latest link in evolution's chain Max
Things will never be the same
You're the first and last
The future and the past—Max

to name a few of them at least from A to Z
There's . . .
Anchiceratops (an-key-SERRA-tops)
Brontosaurus (BRON-tuh-sawr-us)
Columbosauripus (ko-lum-bo-SAWR-ih-pus)
Dimetrodon (dye-MET-ruh-don)
Eryops (ER-ee-ops)
Fabrosaurus (FAB-ruh-sawr-us)

Grallator (GRAL-uh-tor)
Herrerasauridae (her-ray-rah-SAWR-ih-dee)
Iguanodon (ig-WAN-oh-don)
Jaxartosaurus (jax-AR-tuh-sawr-us)
Kentrosaurus (KEN-truh-sawr-us)
Labocania (lab-o-KAY-nee-uh)
Massospondylus (mass-o-SPON-dih-lus)
Nodosauridae (no-doe-SAWR-ih-dee)
Ornithopoda (or-nith-uh-PO-day)
Pentaceratops (PEN-tuh-sair-uh-tops)
Quetzalcoatlus (ket-sol-ko-AT-lus)
Rhamphorhynchus (ram-fo-RINK-us)
Saltoposuchus (salt-o-po-SOOK-us)
Triceratops (try-SAIR-uh-tops)
Ultrasaurus (UL-truh-sawr-us)
Volcanodon (vul-CAN-o-don)
Wuerhosaurus (WER-ho-sawr-us)
Youngoolithus (yung-oo-LITH-us)
Zatomus (zah-TOE-mus)

Now there's us, Now there's us, Now there's us.

Now there's us and we know what there is to know
About these beasts of such colossal size
From bones that we have found and kept
So you can go and stare into a pair of fossil eyes
Then you'll see the mystery of time that passes by
Years and years and years and years under the
    same sky

Then there came Max
The latest link in evolution's chain Max
Things will never be the same
You're the first and last
The future and the past—Max

Note: I could not find a dinosaur name that started
with *X*. A child once suggested I use "Extinctasaurus."

(By permission of Ray Freese)

Marfa Dog

By Ray Freese

I walk the streets, all alone
When I get called, I don't go home
Because I'm, I'm a Marfa Dog
Don't bend down and pat your leg
I don't roll over and I don't beg
Because I'm, I'm a Marfa Dog

Some dogs howl and some dogs bite
Some dogs sleep in the house at night
But I stay underneath the stars
Roamin' free and dodgin' cars

I get back in the early morn'
My master's lookin' so forlorn
She pets my head, treats me well
As I lie down to rest for a spell
And I dream, little puppy dreams

I wake up in the afternoon
She feeds me with a silver spoon
Because I'm, I'm a Marfa Dog
She leaves the house, locks the gate
All I have to do is wait
Because I'm, I'm a Marfa Dog

dogs inside their fence
Lookin' nervous feeling tense
They get real mad, start to growl
As I pass by with a doggy smile

that, Lassie, please do tell?
Timmy's caught down in a well
I'd like to help, but I ain't got time
I'm off to see that bitch of mine

Because I'm, I'm a Marfa Dog
Because I'm, I'm a Marfa Dog
Because I'm, I'm a Marfa Dog

(By permission of Ray Freese)

No Angels in Hell

By Craig Carter and Trent Wilmon

No this ain't Heaven
We're livin' in
You gotta watch for troubles
Around every bend
Between the good and the bad
There's a very thin line
And you'll cross that border
Just to survive

CHORUS:
  I have seen miles
  Of torture and pain
  I've seen the Devil
  Prayin' for rain
  Seen good men buried
  Right where they fell
  You won't see many Angels
  Ridin' through Hell

It's a place for the wicked
A thousand lost souls
Wandering together
Standing alone
And there's no forgiveness
Except by the Son
To die with the righteous
Or live by the Gun

CHORUS:
  Yeah I have seen miles
  Of torture and pain
  I've seen the Devil
  Praying for rain
  Seen good men buried
  Right where they fell
  You won't see many Angels
  Ridin' through Hell

Aiyee yiyee yi
Aiyee yiyee yi
Aiyee yiyee yi
Aiyee yiyee yi

(By permission of Craig Carter)

Lorena

By Craig Carter and Trent Wilmon

We used to meet
At a bend in the river
On the banks
Of the ole Rio Grande
While Mexican moonlight
Played on the water
We silently danced in the sand
Secretly danced in the sand

One stormy midnight
She came to me cryin'
Through teardrops
Tried to explain
How blue Spanish blood
Should not mix with a gringo
And it's forbidden
To see me again
I'll never see you again

CHORUS:
    And I love you Lorena
    The sun always sets in your eyes
    Though shadows have come between us
    Lorena I need you tonight
    I see you when I close my eye aye aye iees

So I headed north
Away from those memories
Tryin' to outride the pain
Stumbled through canyons
Crawled over mountains
Only to find you again
You always find me again

Yo te quiero al modir
Sobre todas las cosas
Tu siempre estarás en mi corazón
Veo tu cara cada vez
Que sueño
Y tengo la misma pasión
Siempre tengo pasión

And I love you Lorena
The sun always sets in your eyes
Though shadows have come between us
Lorena I need you tonight
I see you when I close my eyes
ayieee
Lorena I need you tonight
ayieee
I see you when I close my eyes

(By permission of Craig Carter)

Ride Down the Canyon

CHORUS:
    Ride down the canyon,
    Soar across the ridge,
    Sail the great water,
    Bring your love to me.

I'm riding down the canyon,
Got the wind at my back,
I put in a good day's work,
Now I'm going to find my love.

CHORUS

I'm soaring across the ridge now,
On the wings of a bird,
Flying across the sky now,
To tell you of my love.

CHORUS

I'm sailing the great water,
Being tossed by the waves,
But I'm holding my own course now,
To bring my love to you.

CHORUS

(By permission of Evie Dorsey)

Home to the Chisos

Well, there's fire in the mountains,
A rosy glow around,
Li'l white fluffies in a sky so blue.
And there's green rolling hills,
As far as you can see them,
I wonder why I'm not there with you.

CHORUS:
  I want to go home to the Chisos,
  Those mountains really hold me,
  Home to the land of the Rio Grande.
  I want to go home to the Chisos,
  Those mountains really hold me,
  Home to the land of the ones I love.

I want to be a cowboy's cowgirl,
And ride along beside him,
Riding out in that open range.
I want to be a cowboy's cowgirl,
Sing songs all night,
Making love beneath the stars above.

CHORUS

(By permission of Evie Dorsey)

Springtime in Terlingua

CHORUS:

It's springtime in Terlingua, the buzzards are flying home
The creosote is bloomin' on a hill of broken stone
The sulphur-scented breezes blow around the Rainbow Mine
There's lodes of tailings here and treasure yet to find.

The ghost town comes back to life, now tourism is its game
But in the days of glory past cinnabar was its fame
Perry built his mansion as the workers dug below
No, he never lived there, it was just for show

Short on water, short on wood, the hands moved tons of ore
Paid for their work with scrip good only at Perry's store
The old graveyard stands witness to mining's heavy toll
Their lives slipped by like quicksilver for blasting caps in war

Some say the earth was tired and needed to rest a time
Or cinnabar had run its course, well Perry lost the mine
The wind blows 'cross the desert, it has a timeless sound
It's springtime in Terlingua and new life comes around

(By permission of Chris Müller)

Ramblin' Jack

When I met Ramblin' Jack Elliot I was living in an old ghost town
Down on the border by Mexico where the Rio Grande flows muddy brown
And Jack's stories flowed on like that river in a melodious and raspy sound
Well they say he's not called Ramblin' Jack just because he travels around

Jack told me some tales about Jack Kerouac and Woody Guthrie's old Model A Ford
And how he'd left his autographed copy of *Bound for Glory* on some eighteen wheeler's floorboard
And how on his first trip to Texas back in '52 he ended up in the Houston jail
And when his friend Jerry Garcia died Jack was up in Montana and the heater died in his hotel

CHORUS:
    Ramblin' Jack won't you come on back
    Back to this old Ghost Town
    Down on the border by Mexico where the Rio Grande flows muddy brown
    Hey there Jack won't you please come back
    And rest your ramblin' bones
    Sippin' beer in the shade of The Trading Post
    We'll sing all the old ghost tones

And Jack said he'd stopped by to see Bob Dylan just a few days before in L.A.
He was hoping his old friend and Protégé might come out and listen to him play
Well he says Bob's got him an electric gate, a Vietnamese man and a German dog
None of them spoke any English so Jack just left a note and drove onward through the fog

And Jack told me that he used to be famous, claims he's never even made a dime
And he says the record company's been owing him royalties now for just a goddamn long time
And sometimes he wishes he'd been a trucker instead of ol' Ramblin' Jack
Wearing worn out jeans and cheap tennis shoes, a legend with a load on his back

CHORUS

    And Jack told me he has just two rules in life, before he got in his motorhome rig
    "If you see a side road take it, my friend, and don't you ever be late for your gig"
    Well that side road brought you to this old ghost town, a place you'd been wanting to go
    But Lubbock is a long ways from here, Jack, and I hope you make it in time for your show

(By permission of Laird Considine)

On My Way

CHORUS:
> This is the day, I'm on my way
> This is the day I've been waiting for
> Where I'm going no way of knowing
> All I know is I'm going on my way

I think I've had enough of Austin,
The gigs don't pay and everything's costin' me
I see no reason to stay
It must be time to move along when nothing's right and nothing's wrong
A tank of gas and I'll be on my way

Now all my stuff is in my van, it feels good to be a travelin' man
With the sunshine smiling down on me today
The road behind has set me free and the road ahead is calling me
Somewhere I don't know is on my way

friends out on the Rio Grande say they want me in their band
So maybe I'll just go and check it out
Somewhere there's a place for me and it's someplace I can't wait to be
I'm learning what this living's all about

CHORUS

(By permission of Laird Considine)

Watching a Cactus Bloom

Some say life is empty, some say life is full
Some say life is nothing but a game of push and pull
But life is a gift of mystery that no one really knows
So live it or live with it because it just comes and goes

Some say love is eternal, some say love is dead
Some say love is nothing but some neurons dancing in my head
But love is a gift of mystery that no one really knows
So love it and love with it because it just comes and goes

years of wandering and I'm a long way from the womb
And I'm out here in the desert just watching a cactus bloom

say I've thrown it all away and I've turned my back on life
Some say I've given up on love just because I don't have a wife
Well I filled my life with the stuff some say and then I threw it all away
Now my life is full of loving and the desert's in bloom today

(By permission of Laird Considine)

The Arroyo

The roadrunner crosses the arroyo
Feathers fluffed up in the icy wind
He's looking for nourishment that just isn't there
Winter is such a cruel friend

Hey Roadrunner are you lonely?
Where are you going to sleep if it snows?
I think I could learn about this life from you
Oh, Paisano, there's just so much I want to know
Could you show me where to hide from the storm tonight?

Coyote hunts at night in the arroyo
Singing his song to the freezing wind
He hasn't had much luck on his hunt tonight
Winter is such a cruel friend

Hey Coyote, I love your music
You sing so much better than me
But we both seem to know the same sad song
Would you please sing it with me?
Could you show me how to find my way in this darkness?

The Raven flies over the arroyo
He's laughing as he sails in the wind
He sees all the feathers lying in the snow
Winter is such a cruel friend

Hey Raven, where are you going?
Do you see my teardrops in the snow?
I wish I could fly over this arroyo with you
Oh Cuervo, there's just so much I need to know
Could you show me how to find my way to your laughter?

The man kneels down in the arroyo
And sheltered from the cruel winter wind
He picks up the feathers lying in the snow
And he says good-bye to his friend

(By permission of Laird Considine)

There's a Broken Heart in Big Bend Tonight

Golden Hair Little Girl-splashin' cross a new mowed land
Ridin' Daddy's bronco back-memories long time gone
Soaking wet screaming jet, flying through the rain
Cowgirl Child running wild; Grandma help her with her pain

She rolled into town in a burned out cougar car ride, West Texas mountains calling
In her dreams, burning bridges settin' fire, gonna leave that pain behind,
Terlingua outlaw land there she'll run, there she'll hide

Mountains loomed before her now, like
A castle 'n the sky, Terlingua mi amigo, my friend
Gonna stay here till I die

a broken heart in Big Bend tonight
Terlingua moon shining down will you hold me in your arms?
Tears are runnin' down my face like the mighty Rio Grande
There's a broken heart in Big Bend tonight

Town crazy, Front Porch lazy, eat you up alive
Party town gettin' down, wind erasers steal your mind, slingin' drinks, making tips
Only winners takin' all, happy hour drinking team never heard that one last call

Where's my La Kiva Bar and Grill? Someone took it all away
Oh brother Glenn, I miss your sweet smile, so much I didn't say

Playin' late night show on the Patio, she sat down in front of me, sparkling eyes
Drowning in her deep blue sea, paper flower dance bloomed into romance
You took my breath away, love and music both the same
Please don't leave me baby, oh please stay.

Help me Rhonda if you can, I can't free you from my soul,
Terlingua Creek wash away my pain, agua fria, make me whole again?

CHORUS:
    Terlingua Creek, will you wash away my pain?
    Agua Fria so deep, will you make me whole again?

(By permission of Dr. Fun)

Terlingua Mi Amigo (Terlingua My Friend)

I recall the time when we danced the night away
Down at Boatman's Bar and Grill
Charlie Maxwell, Doug Davis and Chiwawa we all watched the moon stand still
Hey man, you hungry, let me tell you 'bout a feast, down at 3D Deli Diner
Pammy Ware, man, she could throw the food and drove a car like no other

Hot summer days we all swam, load 'em up for Agua Fria
Muddy dogs and ice cold beer, how we laughed at each other
Then came the night that we raised the roof, with my brothers called the "rafters"
Flyin' javelinas, yeah they filled the air, we rocked the night like no other
Terlingua mi amigo, Terlingua my friend
Terlingua mi amigo, Terlingua my friend

A friend in need, well there's help indeed
Hey man, you need a ride?
We've all stood by the graves of those who've gone
How we loved those that died

Terlingua mi amigo, Terlingua my friend
Terlingua mi amigo, Terlingua my friend

Everything gonna be all right, everything gonna be all right
Everything gonna be all right tonight

Terlingua mi amigo, Terlingua my friend
Terlingua mi amigo, Terlingua my friend

¿Dónde va Chupacabra? Ah yo no sé . . .
¿qué pasando?
¡Ah, yo no sé nada!
Ah well, adios pinche gringo
¡Ah bueno!

(By permission of Dr. Fun)

Old Blue Eyes

He's just an old cowboy
With yesterday's dreams
Of wild horses and rodeo queens
And he goes round the country
Pursuing his past
An old cowboy still in his teens
He was a good one
The old timers say
A legend in his own time
You sure would've known it
Had you seen him today
Spurring Nitro out of chute #9
Just two jumps from glory

Old Nitro went down
And we all saw it did not look good
When they called for a doctor
Who knelt by his side
And did for him all that he could
The baritone announcer was silent
As ten thousand fans stood in shock
As that dusty old cowboy opened one squinty blue eye
And said "How's the crowd taking it, Doc?"

Some of them livin,' if they haven't all died
But there's one thing I want you to know
Old Nitro's in Pasture
Producing mean foals
And old Blue Eyes is still riding
The big rodeos.

(By permission of Bake Turner)

Dad

He was born but just a cowboy
Lord, you turned out quite a man
All he knew was "Sure, I can"
Dang near famous for his humor
But his fortune was his hands
He could ride and rope or tell a joke
Much better than any man
He did so many things better
Than a cowboy or a king
But I guess, what he liked best
Was to hear his family sing

He'd blow his old harmonica
'til he ran plumb out of wind
and then he'd be contented
just to slap his knees and grin
I never saw him shed a tear
Although I'm sure he cried
But surely not the way I did the day my best friend died

So Dad, if you're listening, and
I've got a hunch you are,
There's some things I need to tell you
So just lean back on that star.
You're the greatest man I ever knew
And that covers lots of ground
And things 'round here
Just ain't the same
Since you left this little old Texas town
And Dad, the love I have for you
A poet can't describe
But in the dictionary, after sadness
Reads "The day my best friend died."

(By permission of Bake Turner)

ACKNOWLEDGMENTS

THIS BOOK WOULD NOT have been possible without the generosity of the musicians of the Big Bend. They were happy to share their stories and their definitions of the varied genres of music from both sides of the border.

Highly respected musician, songwriter, and guitar maker Michael Stevens of Alpine was the key in ensuring we interviewed a wide range of musicians; just the mention of his name opened many doors for us. Through Michael, we were introduced to the fine performers of the Cowboy Poetry Gathering. He also gathered some musicians together for what is called a "pickin'" session at the Holland Hotel so we could see and hear this assembled group perform informally. It was a delight.

John Ferguson, the mayor of Presidio, arranged our access to the musicians of Ojinaga, Mexico, preserving the unique musical genre called the Ojinaga Sound. He accompanied us on our trips to Ojinaga and acted as our translator in addition to his assistant, the very helpful Stephanie Lares. John was always available for further information about Ojinaga. He has a deep commitment to his Presidio-Ojinaga binational community. His generosity with his time made the Ojinaga interviews possible. We also thank Abraham Baeza, who welcomed us to Ojinaga City Hall. Juan Tarango Martinez provided valuable insights into the passion and sacrifices required to have a life in music from a very early age.

In any book based on interviews, there are some that are not included because of scheduling conflicts and length limitations. Had we been able to include all the interviews we wanted, this would be a multivolume book. Since Bill came from Abilene and I came from El Paso to meet in the Big Bend to work on this book, meeting every two months did make our time limited and dependent on scheduling for both the musicians and us.

Vicki Gibson of Fort Davis did a masterful job in transcribing the interviews and was the definition of grace under pressure.

Thom Lemmons, editor in chief of Texas A&M University Press, made the frequently arduous process of shepherding a manuscript through the publication process resulting in a book an easier one. Even in the midst of a pandemic, he was a center of calm.

His sense of humor and responsiveness to concerns large and small and his outstanding editing skill are much appreciated.

I am most grateful to Bill Wright, award-winning photographer and writer, who is the photographer for *Across the Border and Back: Music in the Big Bend* and my coauthor and photographer for the book *Authentic Texas: People of the Big Bend*. Our collaboration has been a happy and productive one. Bill's brilliant, stunning photographs are the visual half of this book. As a former publisher, I knew that collaborations can often be full of strife, but after twenty-five years as, first, Bill's publisher at Texas Western Press and now with two books behind us, I can say that that was never the case. We have become very familiar with each other's writing styles, serving as the first readers for our other books and offering advice and encouragement. This is what makes our collaborations work.

Bill and I are also grateful for the support and encouragement of our families, especially Howard Daudistel and Alice Everett Wright (1933–2018), who passed away before the completion of the book.

—Marcia Hatfield Daudistel
El Paso, Texas

A NOTE ON THE PHOTOGRAPHS

WHEN MARCIA AND I decided to work on a new book about the Big Bend that would define Big Bend music, I was excited to have a chance to know more about the subject. We had successfully coauthored the book *Authentic Texas: People of the Big Bend* several years ago, so I told her I would be happy to take the photographs for this project. Marcia, an expert storyteller, can also get people to talk about their occupations, lives, and loves. As the project developed, I was amazed at her knowledge of the various musical genres that are the music of the borderlands.

This region constitutes most of the land west of the Pecos River known as Far West Texas to distinguish it from the West Texas that everyone likes to claim from Fort Worth west. Far West Texas has its own appeal to many people: a curiosity for some, an adventure for others, and home for a few.

For years I have photographed people and places in the Big Bend and around the world. In these earlier endeavors I rarely posed a person or groups, preferring to have them sort it out for themselves as long as they stood without unwanted shadows or light that was either too strong or too weak. With this assignment, most of the interviews were conducted where I had little control of the background and lighting. The photos were spontaneous, taken during the interview. Still, I wanted the photographs to clearly portray the subjects' interests and dynamism as they talked to Marcia full of enthusiasm.

In Alpine, Marfa, Fort Davis, Presidio, Marathon, Terlingua, and Ojinaga, Mexico, where Marcia interviewed musicians and I photographed them, they shared their passion for the music of the Big Bend and provided us a rich experience—one that will deeply interest people from metropolitan areas who are unaccustomed to this culture. A stranger might just call this music "country music," but Big Bend music is actually a vast umbrella containing many subdivisions. While my concern was making a photograph that enhanced the story, while listening in on Marcia's discussions, I received quite an education myself. It was a privilege to be asked to provide the visual aspect of the project.

—Bill Wright
Abilene, Texas

DISCOGRAPHY

Craig Carter	*Texas Frontier*
Bill Chappell and Washtub Jerry	*Scorpio Man*
Laird Considine	*Darkness & Lightness*
Declaración Norteña	*Mas Fuertes Que Nunca*
Declaracíon Norteña	*Un Fin de Semana*
Grupo Exito de Marfa, Texas	*Entre Tinieblas*
JUGS	*You Probably Didn't Recognize Me Without My Cape*
Chris McWilliams	*Honeyman*
Chris McWilliams	*Escondido Escapade*
Glenn Moreland	*Glenn Moreland*
Pinche Gringos	*Pinche Gringos*
The Swifts	*Every Day*
Neil Trammell	*Turquoise Troubadour*
Carlos Maxwell and Chihuahua	*No Man's Land*
Scott Walker	*The Rock House Project*
Dr. Fun	*Sanctuary Terlingua*

INDEX